# Hear
## this
## brother

This is the first of a new series of booklets from the *New Statesman*, based on research and writings by *NS* staff and contributors. The best of the *New Statesman* will now be available — updated and expanded — to a wider readership, in paperback form.

Future titles include:

*The Phone-Tappers*
Duncan Campbell on secrets of state surveillance.

*Defence and Disarmament*
Unique collection of disclosure and argument by E.P. Thompson, Robin Cook, Mary Kaldor, Duncan Campbell and others.

*Bad News about the Labour Party*
Analysis of television coverage of Labour's left-right 'split' in 1980, by the Glasgow Media Research Unit.

*Does Parliament Work?*
Examination of the parliamentary and cabinet committee systems by Bruce Page, Frances Wheen, Monica Ferman and others.

*Secret Success of State Industry*
Christopher Hird explains why certain nationalised industries, contrary to popular mythology, are a commercial success.

# Hear this, brother

## Women workers and union power

by **ANNA COOTE** and **PETER KELLNER**
with an Appendix by **JANE STAGEMAN**

# N S Report 1

Anna Coote is Deputy Editor of the *New Statesman*. She writes regularly on women's issues and is co-author with Tess Gill of the Penguin guide to *Women's Rights*. Her other books include *Equal at Work?*, a study of women working in jobs traditionally done by men; *Women Factory Workers*, the case against repealing the protective laws; *Battered Women: a Guide to the New Law*; and *The Rape Controversy*. Before joining the *New Statesman*, she worked for the *Observer* and as a freelance journalist. She studied Modern History and Politics at Edinburgh University, graduating in 1968, and has been active in the women's movement and the trade union movement since the early 1970s.

Peter Kellner is Political Editor of the *New Statesman*. He studied Economics at Cambridge; after graduating in 1969 he joined the staff of the *Sunday Times*. He edited the 'Insight' pages in 1976-7, and in 1978 won the Journalist of the Year award for articles on how Shell and BP evaded oil sanctions against Rhodesia. He is co-author of *Insight on the Middle East War* (1974), *The Year of the Captains: Insight on Portugal* (1975), *Callaghan: The Road to Number Ten* (1976), and *The Civil Servants: an inquiry into Britain's ruling class* (1980). He is married to a full-time working wife, and has two daughters; he insists that he does his full share of cooking, ironing and nappy-changing.

# CONTENTS

# ACKNOWLEDGEMENTS

Our thanks to Market Opinion and Research International for their detailed analysis of workers' attitudes to trade unions (the copyright to the tables in Chapter Three is theirs) and to the *Sunday Times* for allowing us to study unpublished details of MORI polls commissioned by them. We are grateful to Jane Stageman for allowing us to reproduce parts of her study of women trade unionists in the Hull area, as well as her bibliography. For their invaluable help in producing this booklet, thanks to Liz Cooper, Vicky Hutchings and Joanne Hurst.

**Typeset & designed by**
Redesign, 7a Duncan Terrace, London N1.

**Printed by**
Manchester Free Press, 57 Whitworth Street, Manchester 1.

**Published by**
New Statesman, 10 Great Turnstile, London WC1.

ISBN 0 900963 07 0

**Trade distribution by**
Scottish and Northern Book Distribution Ltd.,
18 Granby Row, Manchester 1
&
45/47 Niddry Street, Edinburgh 1.

Southern Distribution
27 Clerkenwell Close, London EC1.

# CHAPTER ONE

# The long fight out of silence

## ANNA COOTE

It was reported in the press one day in 1884 that the town of Kidderminster was 'in an uproar'. The men were all out in the streets

> perambulating . . . with bands and boards on which were drawn men turning mangles and men washing and then came a procession of perambulators wheeled by men, containing infants.

Sad to say, it was not a bid to spend more time helping out at home, but a protest over the employment of women at cheap rates in the local textile industry. The demonstrators were confident that they could make their point by producing the absurd spectacle of men engaged in 'women's work'.

Ninety-one years later, it became illegal for women to be paid less than men for doing the same work. So there has been some progress. It is no longer respectable for male trade unionists to demand openly that women should stay at home and leave the paid jobs to them. Yet today, government policies are designed to encourage just that. Tory ministers — notably Patrick Jenkin — make speeches which convey the very message that the men of Kidderminster were trying to put across in 1884.

Women are not entirely confident that the trade unions will defend their right to work. For they know that men are as terrified as ever at the prospect of 'their' jobs being usurped, and it is abundantly clear that the unions are still run by men. Women workers were organising for better pay and conditions as long ago as the 1820s and for most of the last century they have been trying to gain equal status as trade unionists. Why is it that after so much time and effort, they have gained such a derisory foothold in the labour movement? Some women are put off because the trade unions seem to be a 'man's world' geared to men's needs; and some are too busy to get involved because of their responsibilities at home. But these are symptoms, not causes.

In the late 19th century, women organised their own unions because men would not let them join theirs; gradually, they were absorbed into the men's organisations and this was regarded at the time as a positive achievement. Yet they found that they had simply switched from being first-class members of second-class unions to being second-class members of first-class unions. When the militant and highly successful National Federation of Women Workers, founded by Mary McArthur, voted to join the National Union of General Workers in 1920, it was swiftly submerged: the number of women officials dropped from 16 to one.

Women were relegated then to the margins of trade-union activity and they have stayed there ever since. They are still torn between a desire to be in there with the men, fighting on equal terms, and a knowledge born of bitter experience that they cannot get what they need unless they also organise separately. They hope that by their extra efforts they will win a place at the centre, but the very process of trying has been wearing a rut for them around the periphery.

Women have been marginalised, too, by the measures adopted to improve their pay. For although the trade unions have usually insisted that their goals must be achieved in direct contest with employers, and have fiercely resisted attempts to interfere with collective bargaining, there have been certain exceptions to this rule. From 1918, the lowest-paid and weakest groups of workers (of whom the majority were women) had their wages regulated by statutory bodies known as trade boards. This development was to store up serious problems for the future, as one male delegate to a 1926 TUC conference predicted:

> They [the trade boards] are not in any way encouraging a sense of responsibility among the workers and they are one of the greatest dangers and difficulties we are up against in organising the women. We have to show these people that their only means of improving their condition is by industrial organisation . . .

His warning went unheeded. Wages councils (successors to the trade boards) still govern most sectors of industry where women predominate — and these remain the lowest-paid. Traditional bargaining strategy was again by-passed by the (notoriously ineffective) Equal Pay Act; and women are still seen as a separate class whose needs are not high on the agenda for negotiation.

Then, as now, the aims and strategies of the trade unions were based on two false assumptions: first, that paid employment is *real* work while domestic labour and child care are not; and second, that the latter are naturally the province of women while men have an inalienable right to whatever paid jobs are going. During two world wars, women were called to do their patriotic duties in the factories of Britain, but as soon as the men returned from the front they were dispatched back to their kitchens. In 1947, the TUC annual report announced that there was no doubt in the General Council's mind

> that the home is one of the most important spheres for a woman worker and that it would be doing a grave injury to the life of the nation if women were persuaded or forced to neglect their domestic duties in order to enter industry particularly where there are young children . . .

The men of Kidderminster seemed to march again. And their ghosts still stalk the corridors of Congress House. As paid work becomes scarcer, so women's unpaid domestic labour grows magically more vital to the life and health of the nation. But somehow male trade unionists never imagine any serious increase in their own contribution to the nurturing of future generations. By insisting that this is women's work, they justify their own prior claim to paid jobs and so maintain economic power as breadwinners-in-chief. 'Let us be honest,' said Pat Turner, women's organiser of the GMWU, to the 1972 TUC:

> The right to work is not generally considered a female prerogative. Women are still considered a reliable safety margin for an unreliable labour market which we can use when we have need of them and can disregard all other times.

Her words are just as true today.

(Based on a review of *Women Workers and the Trade Unions*, Sarah Boston (Davis-Poynter) in *New Statesman*, 25 July 1980.)

## CHAPTER TWO

# Powerlessness
# and how to fight it

## ANNA COOTE

*'If you ask me,' said the male shop steward, 'women are their own worst enemy.
If I was a women in this factory and I wanted to put up for convenor, I'd feel sure
I was going to walk it. There's 300 women on the books here and only 70 men . . .
Mind, you don't want to change a good person just because you want to put a
woman in, do you?'*

*'I must say, I despair of our girls sometimes,' the senior woman official
confided. 'They just don't seem to be interested in the union. There's nothing to
stop them getting involved. I've never had any trouble, the men treat me just
like one of them. Women have only got themselves to blame if they don't
put themselves forward.'*

*'It wouldn't make any difference if there were more female shop stewards,'
said the woman on the shopfloor. 'Why should it? The union treats you the same
whether you're a man or a woman. I mean, I'm paying my 35p the same as any
man. They've got to treat you equal!'*

Cathy, the shop floor worker quoted above, described to me the grading system
in the glass factory where she worked, on the outskirts of Liverpool. Out of nine
grades, the women were concentrated in the lower four. She felt particularly
strongly about her own job, which involved stamping the glasses as they came
off the assembly line; it was in grade three. 'We should be in grade seven.
Machine operators are in grade six and it's an easier job. The ones in our room,
if the machine's running smoothly, they can sit there all morning and read a
paper, while I put in four and a half hours, continuously, like a robot.'
Cathy couldn't recall who had organised the grading system. She guessed
the management alone had been responsible, although in fact it was negotiated
with the unions. Could her union get her on to a higher grade? She shook her
head: 'They've tried.' Had they tried hard enough? (Pause . . .) 'Well they can't

have, can they, because we're still on grade three!' Her assumption that her union *had* to treat women and men as equals — because it said it did, or because it ought to — did not tally with her knowledge of the way the fruits of collective bargaining were distributed at her workplace.

Cathy belongs to the General and Municipal Workers Union, of whose 956,000 members, more than a third are female. Yet in 1981 it has no women at all on its 40-strong national executive committee; of its 243 officials, 13 are women; and only three of its 73 delegates to the 1980 Trades Union Congress were female.

# Women in the unions

*Figures in brackets show how many women there would be if they were represented according to their share of the membership.*

| Union | Membership | | | Executive Members | | Full time Officials | | TUC Delegates | |
|---|---|---|---|---|---|---|---|---|---|
| | Total | F | %F | Total | F | Total | F | Total | F |
| APEX (Professional, Executive, Clerical, Computer) | 150,000 | 77,000 | 51% | 15 | 1(8) | 55 | 2(28) | 15 | 4(8) |
| ASTMS (Technical, Managerial) | 472,000 | 82,000 | 17% | 24 | 2(4) | 63 | 6(11) | 30 | 3(5) |
| BIFU (Banking, Insurance, Finance) | 132,000 | 64,000 | 49% | 27 | 3(13) | 41 | 6(20) | 20 | 3(10) |
| GMWU (General & Municipal) | 956,000 | 327,000 | 34% | 40 | 0(14) | 243 | 13(83) | 73 | 3(25) |
| NALGO (Local Govt Officers) | 705,000 | 356,000 | 50% | 70 | 14(35) | 165 | 11(83) | 72 | 15(36) |
| NUPE (Public Employees) | 700,00 | 470,000 | 67% | 26 | 8(17) | 150 | 7(101) | 32 | 10(22) |
| NUT (Teachers) | 258,000 | 170,000 | 66% | 44 | 4(29) | 110 | 17(73) | 36 | 7(24) |
| UNTGW (Tailor & Garment) | 117,000 | 108,000 | 92% | 15 | 5(14) | 47 | 9(43) | 17 | 7(16) |
| TGWU (Transport & General) | 2,070,000 | 330,000 | 16% | 39 | 0(6) | 600 | 6(96) | 85 | 6(14) |
| USDAW (Shop, Distributive Allied) | 462,000 | 281,000 | 63% | 16 | 3(10) | 162 | 13(102) | 38 | 8(24) |
| TOTALS | 6,022,000 | 2,265,000 | 38% | 316 | 40(150) | 1,636 | 90(640) | 418 | 66(174) |

*All figures are approximate, and the most recent that were available in November 1980.*

The GMWU is no exception, as the table shows. Nor is Cathy's predicament unusual. In most work places in Britain, women are concentrated in the lower-paid grades — and this often fails to reflect the value of their work. It isn't hard to detect a link between the two factors: if women are not active in their unions, their needs are less likely to be given priority in the course of collective bargaining. But it is far more difficult to isolate the causes. *Why* don't women exercise power in the union in proportion with their numbers? What's holding them back?

The *New Statesman*/MORI poll, described by Peter Kellner in Chapter 3, suggests there are only minimal differences between male and female attitudes towards employment and trade unionism. Generally speaking, it looks as though women are satisfied with their lot and, should they wish to play a more active role, men are not bent on blocking their way. These findings are echoed in the remarks of the male shop steward and the senior female official at the beginning of this chapter. However, my own investigations, backed up by what little research has been done in this country, suggest there are more complex feelings beneath the surface.

Most women who experience unfair pay and powerlessness have scarcely begun to articulate these problems as a grievance, let alone to identify solutions to them. When I talked to Cathy, together with three of her workmates, it was the first time any of them had discussed the link between their pay and their own participation — as women — in the union. After two hours of mulling the question over they were seeing things in quite a different light. (And I swear I fed them no lines!) Early in the meeting, one said emphatically that men should be paid more than women; the conversation turned to redundancies (two were afraid their husbands would lose their jobs), and to the grading system in the factory; after some 20 minutes, I reminded her of what she had said. 'No: scratch that. Because nowadays you get a lot of women on their own, and women left working when their husbands are put out of work. I never really gave that thought before.'

## Beyond the 'general problem'

In some circumstances men, too, suffer from unfair pay and powerlessness — at a workplace where the union is poorly organised, for instance, or where the wages of one group have fallen behind those of another. Men, too, can be reluctant to air their grievances. Men, too, can find themselves cut off from the centres of activity and authority in their unions. Most people would now agree that there are fundamental difficulties about the way the trade unions are organised, which affect all members, male and female. How should the unions cope with the volume of their membership, with the scope and complexity of their business? How can they create and maintain a (seemingly impossible) synthesis of democracy, unity, power and efficiency? If the right answers were found, they would surely help women overcome their present impotence. But that is not the end of the matter. The fact remains that for all the inadequacies of the trade union movement, it is men, not women, whose voice is heard, whose strength is felt, whose investment in the organisation yields the greater dividends.

It has been the main task of the trade unions for more than a century to meet the needs of male workers. They are therefore relatively well-equipped to identify their problems and find solutions for them. By contrast, the reasons why women are low-paid and powerless are diverse and complicated, ranging far beyond the economic relationship between workers and employers. They are not a familiar part of trade union language (Spender, 1980). There are no established channels for talking about them. There is no bank of experience on which to draw to meet the needs of working women.

A useful comparison can be drawn with black workers. Like women, they occupy the lower-paid jobs and their voice is scarcely heard in the unions. In their case, too, the reasons for their low pay and powerlessness are complicated and cannot be explained in class terms alone. And while the problems of women and ethnic minorities are by no means the same, lessons can be learned and exchanged between the two groups.

## Forming the habit of power

Sarah Boston has recorded the long and frustrating struggle of women to gain
an equal voice in the unions (Boston, 1980). As she points out, it is not that men
have conspired to keep women down; it is just that the machinery they have set
up to improve their wages and conditions has time and again failed to accom-
modate the needs of women. The campaign for the Equal Pay Act was supported
by the unions, yet it amounted to an admission that collective bargaining would
not give women a fair deal; it was an (unsuccessful) attempt to circumvent the
problem.

By tradition, trade union bargaining has rested on the idea that men have
a right to earn a 'family wage', and although this has seldom reflected the economic reality of most households, it has left women hanging on to the edge of
trade unionism, as marginal and intermittent wage earners. Seeing themselves
as 'breadwinners', male unionists concentrate their demands on wages, rather
than on other factors. They also tend to believe, for the same reason, that
women's jobs are less important than theirs, requiring not only lower priority
in the pay queue and less vigorous protection from redundancy, but also
continuing support from men.

Women's additional tasks of child rearing and housekeeping have never
been considered the proper concern of trade unions — even though wages could
not have been earned without them. And since women have had no alternative
means of getting together and discussing their needs, they have come to accept
the dominant view of what is important and reasonable, and what is not. At the
same time, the dominant view remains a rather alien one — which helps to
explain why women can present one set of attitudes on initial questioning (as
in the MORI poll) and another after they have had a chance to talk things over
with each other for a while.

In a pharmaceutical factory in the north-west, I met the seven female stewards there. Like the women in Cathy's factory, they had never before met
together as a group. They outnumbered the men in the factory by more than four
to one, yet the men clearly ran the union. The women were paid no more than
the lowest male grade, but they worked far more intensively than most of the
men.

'Like at break time in the afternoon we've got ten minutes,' one explained.
'The women are on the line and the buzzer goes. You run the length of the
factory, up four flights of stairs, run right down to the canteen, get a drink, sit
down, scald your tonsils and you've got to be back on the line before the buzzer
blows. The men, they saunter in and saunter out. If we're late back, it's marked
down on the lost time paper, but they're not as hard on the men. The management bends over backwards towards the men.'

Why was that? 'The men all stick together. We find a lot of women don't —
they split up.'

Later, three male stewards joined the discussion. 'The reason men are
strong in the union,' said one, 'is because we get together. The women are tied
on the line, they can't stop. There's plenty of time during the day when we

can all get together. Quite often all the men are in one cloakroom.' Couldn't the women get together at lunch time? Apart from practical difficulties — they were on different shifts and (as one said) the married women had to go out shopping — it hadn't occurred to them: the men gathered in the cloakrooms during the day just as they gathered in the pubs as night. I was left with the firm impression that if the women developed a similar habit, their strength would be enormous. For they were neither docile, nor down-trodden, nor disinclined to unity. Nor were they slow to recognise their predicament. They were just beginning to find their feet.

## Unfamiliar territory

In all the things a woman must do to be active and influential in her union (attending meetings and courses, knowing rules and procedures, speaking out in public, taking on the management), she must operate under terms and conditions laid down by men, whose experience and preoccupations may differ quite profoundly from her own. Thus, it is common for a woman to hang back, or give up altogether, while her male equivalent will have a go, bluff his way through, in what seems to him to be more familiar territory. Doris, a shop steward at the Merseyside glass factory, told me there'd never been a female convenor there, and wouldn't ever be, as far as she could tell. 'I don't know why. It's a big responsibility. It is for a feller, I know, but a woman, like, wouldn't say the things that a feller says.' What sort of things? 'You know, the way they talk to management, I think a woman would be a bit more timid.' Would *she* be timid? She thought so, but her workmates all disagreed. 'Once she gets going, no.' 'Doris speaks for us in our room when we have arguments and if someone's out of turn she'll say "shurrup and let me say what I want to say".' 'She can speak for herself and for us.' 'It's confidence, isn't it?'

In Jane Stageman's study of female trade unionists in the Hull area, outlined in Appendix Two, 108 women from five branches (spanning the private and public sector, services and manufacturing) answered questions about the obstacles they perceived to their greater participation in union affairs. The questions were split up in an attempt to isolate 'personal', union-related and job-related factors: the first two categories elicited by far the largest response. Under the 'personal' heading, 44 per cent said 'feeling more confident' would encourage participation, and this was surpassed only by 'having a greater interest in union affairs' and 'fewer home responsibilities', at 56 and 55 per cent. The latter response was echoed by many of the women I interviewed.

Julie, one of the stewards at the pharmaceutical factory, pointed out that it was all very well for men to go off to union meetings, but they were outside working hours: 'As you know, a lot of women have to go home and cook the tea for their husbands. Or they can't get out because they've got to do their ironing and their washing.'

Some said their husbands would disapprove if they knew they were going to a pub for a union meeting. But most striking of all was the link between the prospect of 'responsibility', which deterred so many women from holding union office, and the role they played at home. It was not simply that women had less time: they were reluctant to add to the mental and emotional burden — of looking after other people's interests, having to remember to do things, always being on call — which they already carried with their domestic responsibilities. And they generally didn't recognise that the experience of dealing with a home and family could be a real asset to a union activist. One member said she thought women didn't make good shop stewards because they lost their tempers more quickly than men. 'I'm very short-tempered. I think I'd get more worked up than a man would.' Did she lose her temper at home with her children? 'No never! If they get on my nerves that much I do go away, calm down, then come back and start again.' On reflection she agreed that a woman could learn to cope with management just as she learned to cope with her kids: it was all down to experience.

Jane Stageman points out that the hierarchies of trade unions reflect the hierarchies in employment. Women are accustomed to being at the bottom of the pile, behaving deferentially towards men and expecting little or no advancement. This is bound to shape their aspirations and expectations in trade union affairs. Moreover, says Stageman:

> The fact that the interests of men and women were generally different in every branch [in her study] was ensured by the sexual division of labour operating in . . . the sectors of employment where the unions were organising.

She found no evidence, however, 'of action being taken . . . to attempt to erode these occupational divisions between the sexes, despite the fact that women members showed most concern over this aspect of their employment position.'

## A conflict of interest

Her findings support the evidence provided by the London School of Economics' equal pay project, which monitored 26 organisations between 1974 and 1977, to see what effect the Equal Pay and Sex Discrimination Acts were having (Snell, 1979). The LSE results show the remarkable lengths to which employers had gone to minimise their obligations under the Equal Pay Act — from altering the content of men's and women's jobs to avoid 'like work' comparisons and restructuring grading systems to leave women in the lowest grades, to altering factors by which jobs were evaluated to favour those done by men, and giving men additional duties to justify restoring differentials. Employers were found to be affected by fears of reactions from men and lack of pressure from unions:

> In amost every case, management conceded the men's demands in order to avoid possible disruption and conflict . . . In several cases, unions actively colluded with management to minimise [their obligations] or allowed management to carry out such actions without protest.

Under the Sex Discrimination Act, 'changes have been few and on the whole superficial'. In more than half the organisations studied, managers admitted they were discriminating against women; but no cases had been taken up —

either directly to tribunals or through trade union negotiation. Women sometimes knew they were victims of discrimination, but did not pursue the matter:

> The reasons given were fears of unpleasantness and disruption at work, the
> difficulty of proving a case, the feeling that it was not worth the trouble
> involved and lack of support from the union. For example, union represent-
> atives in one organisation dismissed women's complaints of discrimination
> with the statement that it was 'management's right to select whoever they
> like'.

The LSE researchers concluded that active involvement by trade unions at the
workplace could have a tremendous impact on pay and opportunities for women
— by monitoring management practices, identifying inequalities and pressing
for change — and that this could have far more effect than simply amending the
laws. What was more:

> The project findings make it clear that women's greater involvement in
> unions and pay determination is essential if women are to safeguard their
> interests at work.

Why is it that men — who have the power to act, while women are still
excluded from power — do so little to change the status quo? It cannot just be
lethargy, since they are often found to be busy resisting change. Why, then?

Trade unions still operate according to the principles on which they were
originally founded: to protect their members' interests. Inevitably, the strongest
unions, or the strongest groups within unions, are most successful, in the
normal run of industrial affairs, at protecting their own interests. The history
of trade unionism is rich with brave acts of comradeship, but *pure* altruism,
which involves self-denial without future gain, has never been a *primary*
function and seldom enters into collective bargaining. The thousands of workers
who supported the Grunwick strike (for example) felt that the struggle of those
Asian workers was their struggle too. But at this stage, men do not identify
with the struggle of women in the same way.

As trade unionists, men have always had more muscle than women, and
most of them suspect that they have nothing to gain and possibly much to lose
by promoting equal pay and opportunity for women. They feel this more strongly
than ever when the job market is contracting and when money is short. It could
be said that in the long term men's lives will be improved by sex equality, but
arguments of that kind are complex and rather abstract and don't carry much
weight with the average male worker. In the immediate sense, then, there is a
genuine conflict of interest.

Women workers may have been reluctant to look too closely at the reasons
why men fail to support them. They have to live with them, after all. It cannot
be easy to confront a conflict of interest with men at work while building a
domestic life on an assumption of common interest. Men have no particular
incentive to examine their own motives or seek to change themselves in this
respect. But the conflict won't be resolved unless it is recognised.

## Tokens, ghettos and insults

There have been fierce arguments for at least two decades about what should be done to get women more involved in trade union activities. Should there be special conferences, special courses, special committees, special seats? Or would these amount to tokenism; would they ghettoise women's issues; would they insult women by treating them as something other than exact equals of men? When I first attended the annual TUC women's conference in 1977, I witnessed its (last) narrow escape from abolition: certain unions were arguing that the Sex Discrimination Act had heralded a new era of equality which made a separate conference at best superfluous, at worst a dangerous diversion. But they lost, and since then more and more unions have been experimenting with special measures of various kinds.

The white collar engineers' union TASS appointed a national women's organiser as early as 1974; it has women's sub-committees at national and divisional levels, each with a special seat on its parent body; it runs an annual weekend women's school; and it produces an impressive range of literature on issues of special concern for women. TASS now has a large and vocal contingent of female activists. The National Union of Public Employees has created five seats for women on its national executive, acknowledging that women's under-representation has nothing 'to do with "women's nature" or lack of interest in the affairs of NUPE [but] . . . with the position of women in the wider society and at work.' The local government officers' union NALGO has a network of equal opportunities committees and a regular equal opportunities bulletin, while (somewhat contradictorily) refusing to send delegates to the TUC women's conference. Two other white collar unions, APEX and ASTMS have similar arrangements for national and regional committees; and the two largest blue-collar unions, the Transport and General and the GMWU, have recently resolved to set up equal rights committees in their regions.

In 1981 the TUC women's advisory committee increased the number of its members elected by the women's conference from eight to ten (the remaining nine are appointed by the General Council); and the General Council increased its women's section from two to five seats (instead of seven, as requested by the TUC women's conference). In 1979, Congress endorsed a 10-point charter, *Equality for Women within Trade Unions*, urging unions to take positive steps to encourage women's participation. It recommends, where appropriate, women's seats on national and local bodies, special advisory committees, paid time off for union meetings in working hours, child care arrangements for meetings, special encouragement for women to attend union training, and non-sexist union publications. (The Charter is reproduced in full in Appendix 1.)

Perhaps the most important development in the last two or three years has been the recognition by many unions that the problem (of women's powerlessness) is a long-term one: we are not poised on the brink of true equality, we are just starting to climb the hill towards it. My own union, the NUJ, set up an Equality Working Party in 1975, with a double brief to promote equality in journalism and fight sexism in the media. In subsequent years vigorous efforts were made to disband it — and while some of its opponents were driven simply by a distaste for equality, others sincerely believed that *the job was nearly done*. By 1981, the Working Party seemed at last to be convincing members that male dominance is so deeply entrenched that it will take many decades to eradicate it; and that more, not fewer, special measures are needed to speed the process.

This pattern is apparently being repeated in other unions — as the truth (unpalatable to some) begins to emerge that the more unions do to encourage women, the more conscious women will become of their potential, and the more they will demand. In November 1980, the TUC held a special conference on positive action. The delegates were in no doubt about the need for special measures; the speeches were all about *which* measures they should adopt and what lessons could be learned from the experience of others.

Increasingly, too, women are tracing the links between their lack of power and their own domestic arrangements. And they are beginning to insist that this is a matter for the unions to take up — since what happens to women inside the home affects their ability to win proper rewards for their labour outside the home. As one speaker at the TUC conference put it: 'When will *our* unions start telling *our* members to do their fair share of work at home, so that *our* members can get out to meetings?'

It is still assumed that male workers operate in a sphere which is separate from the home, while women workers, though they may go each day to the same factory or office, occupy another sphere which incorporates the home. Valerie Charlton and Beatrix Campbell have pointed out that men's strategy in collective bargaining 'historically has not expressed any responsibility as *active* fathers, because they have none' (Campbell, Charlton, 1978).

If men saw themselves as full-time, active parents (as women do, even when they're in full-time employment), with a commitment to their families in terms of time and energy rather than primarily in terms of cash, they might view their interests from a new perspective. It isn't inconceivable, for instance, that a man would *want* to devote more attention to his kids — especially if he had more time and was under less pressure to earn money. He might thus come to see more relevance in fighting for shorter hours, equal pay, child care provisions and parental leave. This would not only transform the character of collective bargaining, but also help right the balance of power between men and women in the unions.

## Does positive action work?

It is hard to assess the results so far of the various measures unions have adopted, although broad lessons can be drawn from them. Equality working parties and women's advisory committees can meet for years on end, campaigning hard and producing first-rate literature, yet fail to get their message through to more than a minority of members. Communication is likely to be especially poor if the union is large, with members scattered around small workplaces and with no centralised bargaining structure. When I met two groups of female GMWU members in the north of England, I asked them three questions: Did their union have a national officer with special responsibility for women? Did their region have an equal rights officer? Had there recently been an equal rights conference in their area? In each case, all of them answered with an emphatic — and inaccurate — 'NO'. But it would be unfair to focus on the difficulties of the GMWU, which are no greater than average. A group of NUPE women in the south-east could not tell me the names of any of their female national executive members.

Jane Stageman confirms that poor communication is a major obstacle to women's participation: 62 per cent of the members she questioned thought women would be encouraged if union matters were 'made easier to understand'; and 56 per cent thought it would help if more information were available about how their unions worked. In her paper, *Women in ASTMS*, Marjorie Harrison points to the crucial role of branch secretaries (Harrison, 1980). The ASTMS National Women's Advisory Committee had been worried by the lack of response to a letter sent out to members, and so arranged a follow-up:

> It was discovered that some Secretaries were not passing on the information at all and others, instead of reading from the letter (which was deliberately low key) were mentioning almost in passing that 'two women's libbers want to come and talk to you about women's lib', which got the reaction it was geared to receive — rejection.

Harrison, herself an activist in ASTMS, studied the impact of her union's advisory committee and concluded that its greatest measurable achievements were in helping to preserve abortion rights, and other 'social issues' such as the campaign for child benefit. On industrial matters such as pay and maternity leave, its impact had been minimal, because it had no direct links with the officials responsible for negotiations. The ASTMS experience is typical of many unions. A strong distinction remains between 'women's issues' and industrial matters; special measures adopted so far have failed to increase women's involvement in the latter sphere, where men remain in control. This suggests some new strategies will have to be devised.

There are few signs that special women's committees are increasing the level of female representation on unions' national and regional bodies. (They many in the long-term, but progress is slow.) After years of campaigning for equality in the NUJ, I paid my first visit to our national executive committee in 1980 to discuss an item on the agenda. It was not a pretty sight: a large room, a horseshoe arrangement of tables and a solid line of male faces, broken only by a solitary female at the far end — the minutes secretary. Of course I had known there were no women members, but as a spectacle it had a surprisingly powerful effect. (Should there be regular sightseeing visits for all women in the NUJ?)

The majority of opinion in my union seems to be against reserved seats for women (on 'tokenism' grounds), but I am not convinced. NUPE's experiment is said to have encouraged the election of three additional women on to its executive. But at the same time there is evidence that in NUPE links are weak between the women who hold special seats on the executive on the one hand, and the ordinary female members and the business of policy-making on women's issues on the other. These links might be strengthened if the women on the executive were also representatives of a network of national and regional women's committee. (So far NUPE has no such network.)

Of course, the sizes and structures of unions vary considerably. A small, fairly centralised union such as AUEW (TASS) or ASTMS can implement measures to encourage women more quickly and effectively than a giant like the Transport and General Workers' Union. The T&G is proud of its internal democracy and insists that measures cannot be imposed from the top. When its 1979 biennial delegate conference voted to set up regional equal rights committees, it could not *instruct* the regions how and when to do so. Each one went about the job in its own way — and the results have been very patchy. Prohibitive postal costs mean that information from head office has to be filtered down in batch-mailings through regions and districts to branches and shop stewards. The T&G has the third largest female membership in the country, yet at almost every point in its massive hierarchy, men are firmly in control. There are no women on its national executive. The influence of the few officials who are genuinely committed to equality can seldom penetrate beyond their own localities. On the one hand, therefore, the size of the T&G is such that it may require more urgent and sweeping measures than other unions, yet on the other hand, its unwieldy bulk is likely to inhibit such developments. Democracy is a good thing and needs all the encouragement it can get in the trade union movement. But women represent only 16 per cent of the T&G's total membership: how is the need to proceed democratically to be reconciled with the need to promote progressive measures which serve the interests of a minority?

NALGO, which is the fourth-largest union, with the second-largest female membership, does not have the same difficulties, and women are far more vocal there, for several reasons. It is organised around large bargaining centres (local authorities, water boards, etc.), which means that communication is easier; women represent half the total membership; and it's a white-collar union. There is evidence (some of which is described by Peter Kellner in the next chapter) of more progressive attitudes to equality among white-collar workers. That said, it is important to point out that women are still conspicuously under-represented in NALGO.

## The impact of the activist

Whatever the size or character of a union, there is no doubt that forceful individuals can have a big impact on female awareness and solidarity. Marjorie Harrison claims that one particular woman was able to swing the entire ASTMS executive from opposing to supporting the setting-up of a woman's advisory committee. Marjorie Mayo and others, who have studied the union involvement of home helps and meals-on-wheels workers in the London borough of Tower Hamlets (Wigram, 1980), conclude that attendance at union meetings 'was considerably better where there was an active shop steward on the premises to keep members informed and call sectional meetings where necessary'. And at London's Heathrow Hotel, an ebullient Spanish woman, Marisa Casares-Roach, has changed the face of the Transport and General Workers' Union.

Marisa, a former waitress and swimming pool attendant, joined the union five years ago and is now the convenor, with 360 members, half of whom are women. From being in a minority of one, she has reached the point where there are nine female and three male stewards (and, as she points out, the organisation couldn't have survived if she hadn't retained the support of all her members). 'Women make better shop stewards,' she says. 'They are more inclined to understand people's problems, they can *sense* things. And they have more patience, too.' Over the years she has kept an eye out for potential stewards, then coaxed each one painstakingly into the job. 'Of course they don't think they can do it at first. You just have to show them they can, and stay with them. But you couldn't rely on a man to do that.'

Marisa sets great store by union training courses, on the ground that knowledge is sure to bring confidence, and she takes the view that child care facilities should be provided at all of them (she has two young children). Through the training courses, she also builds contacts with female activists in other parts of the country, and keeps in touch by telephone afterwards. Her achievements suggest how much could be done if unions appointed more full-time female organisers. And the value of support networks — formal and informal — cannot be underestimated, in view of the extraordinary pressures to which female activists are exposed.

Because of their rarity, women whose heads emerge above the crowd are swiftly burdened with responsibility; and they often have extra commitments (to women's meetings as well as to their families), on top of all their regular union duties. The higher up the ladder they go, the more isolated they become and the tougher it gets to prove they can do the job. It is common for women who hold senior office to find they have no more time for their equal rights or women's advisory committees. Some who get near the top, having fought for most of their lives to 'make it' on men's terms, get comfy as token women and lose sight of their sisters' need for a helping hand. Some hold on to their commitment, but are driven in their isolation to degrees of paranoia and over-caution. These problems will only diminish if the support networks grow stronger; if more women emerge in senior positions; and if union hierarchies keep in much closer touch with the grass roots.

## The catalytic effect of getting together

For the women who are just setting out, recent trade union experiments with various forms of 'positive action' suggest that two measures in particular could have a profound effect. The first is to ensure that women's domestic responsibilities don't stop them getting to union meetings. The most effective way is to negotiate work-time meetings, and Jane Stageman's study confirms that more women see this as a spur to activism than anything else. But it wouldn't suit all workplaces and, where it doesn't, it is essential to provide for child care — either by laying on a creche, or by arranging baby-sitting payments.

The second measure — which promises to be the most catalytic — is to give women plenty of opportunity to meet together *as women*. This is a difficult point to argue (outside feminist circles), because the effect really has to be witnessed to be appreciated. I know that many who attend the TUC women's conference find it of immeasurable value just to be in a room with other women, discussing issues of special concern to them without — as it were — looking over their shoulders. There is always a remarkable degree of unanimity (the women *know* what they want, they just haven't got the power to achieve it); and there is often a faint buzz of euphoria, because it is such a rare experience for women to meet together in those numbers.

I recently visited a NUPE weekend school, arriving on Sunday afternoon after 25 women — nurses, caterers, cleaners, a road sweeper, a gardener and others — had been together for 36 hours. It had been a novel occasion for all of them and they, too, were euphoric (even though they had been up half the night boozing and bopping and playing silly games, and they had terrible hangovers). It wasn't just that they'd had a good time, although that was important enough; they'd spent the daytime learning how to negotiate and discussing their common and separate experiences. They had evidently found it invaluable. Now they said they wanted more courses like this one; they wanted to learn more and they wanted to see each other again. What had they discovered that was new? 'Not *new*, exactly,' said one. 'It's things I've had in my head all the time, but I thought it was just *me!*' 'We couldn't have spoken freely if men had been here,' another said. 'We need a few more of these, and then we could go on a mixed course. We've got to get ourselves more educated — we're only on the edge.'

In 1980, the NUJ had its first conference for women — after three years' campaigning to make it happen. It was generally regarded as a rare, one-off occasion. More than 200 women came, and because it was open, rather than a delegate conference (the union paid fares), many of them had previously had little or no contact with the NUJ beyond their own chapels. At the end of the day the overwhelming feeling was that it had not been long enough. The women all said they wanted regular conferences — preferably as a two-day, annual event. Whether the union will agree to such an outrageous demand remains to be seen!

Much to its credit, the TUC has started organising special courses for women. Jenny Owen has been running them in the Manchester and Liverpool areas. 'It works every time,' she told me. 'They all say it makes such a difference to have just women on their own, and at the end of two days they're high on it.' It is that sense of solidarity which women need to nurture, and carry with them into the heart of trade union affairs.

## Up against the Tories

Not that it will be easy in the political and economic climate of the early 1980s. When short-time, redundancy and closures are threatened, unions concentrate on saving jobs rather than promoting equality, and gains that women have made can be swept away. In October 1980 I went to interview a T&G shop steward in Hayes, Middlesex. Jakinder, an Indian woman in her early 30s, had helped organise workers (mainly women) in a small seat-belt factory, and she described — with some passion — the changes which had overcome the place. They had won better pay, proper heating and an end to arbitrary lay-offs; the union was a force to be reckoned with; the management respected her and so did the workers. She was very happy; it was the first time she had been involved in union activity. But the day before I met her, they'd all been put on a one-day week. The management said there were no more orders. In a stroke, the union was undermined; they'd lost their bargaining power. Jakinder was now beset with worries about losing her job — and there seemed to be nothing she could do to help herself or her fellow workers.

Many thousands of women and men are suffering a similar fate — and there are rumblings in some quarters about the need for men to have the first claim on jobs, while women return to the home. True, women bear children from time to time. But it is also true that for most of their adult lives women need to earn a living to support themselves and their families. In a period of recession, therefore, it is no less vital for women's voice to be heard in the unions, it is simply more difficult. And indeed, if they are to protect their hard-won rights, they will need to assert themselves all the more forcefully.

## Try everything

At the TUC's positive action conference in November 1980, many delegates stressed the problem of finding the *right* measure to suit the character of their own organisations. Two unions have commissioned studies of themselves from Warwick University, and these have led to proposals for particular steps to encourage women's participation (one was for NUPE and led to the special seats on its executive). Academic studies can be useful in identifying general structural problems, and in providing information about the extent of women's involvement; they can certainly help to legitimise the subject as a matter of concern. However, I doubt if there is any real mystery (requiring academic scrutiny) about what unions should do if they want to increase women's activity. There are plenty of tried and tested methods — and each union probably needs to try *all* of them over a reasonable period of time: reserved seats, networks of advisory committees and special officers, equal rights conferences, extra training sessions, workplace discussion groups, single-sex meetings, leaflets, posters, pamphlets and campaigns. These need to be arranged in such a way as to have a maximum impact on the broad membership of the union, as well as on its power-lines and policy-makers — and here a Warwick-style study could come in handy. As the effects are monitored, so the next steps can be devised.

All the evidence suggests that where one strategy (such as NUPE's special seats, or the GMWU's equal rights committees) seems to be having too little impact, that is because it is not backed up by other measures (such as training courses, publicity campaigns and improved communication). Everything that has been tried so far has succeeded to *some* extent, however limited, in shedding more light on the special needs of women, and in bringing more women into the mainstream of union affairs. The more measures a union adopts, the faster its progress. Women are unlikely to be antagonised or intimidated, provided the measures are presented in terms which relate to their own experience. Of course, they take time to adapt to new opportunities; changes in the level of their activism must be expected to occur over half and whole decades, rather than over months or years.

The question, therefore, is not *which* measures encourage women, for they all do; but how can unions do all that is necessary to develop women's power in proportion with their numbers *and* retain the loyalty and enthusiasm of their male members? An academic study could perhaps be commissioned, on the assumption that every available measure will be taken to increase female participation, with the aim of finding out how best to encourage men to adjust to the changes that will ensue.

# CHAPTER THREE

# The working woman: her job, her politics and her union

## PETER KELLNER

Before the Second World War, Britain's labour force was remarkably stable. At any given moment about 14 million men and 5 million women either had jobs or were looking for work. Political emancipation for women after the First World War did not lead to immediate economic emancipation: indeed, if anything, the 1920s saw a slight decline in the numbers of women at work. It was not until the late 1930s, when the British economy was recovering from the depression, that the number of women in the labour force started to grow noticeably. At the outbreak of the Second World War, six million women were working — one million more than a decade earlier.

During the war, of course, the number of working women rose sharply, reaching almost nine million in 1943. Although the number fell again in the late 1940s as servicemen were demobbed, the underlying trend remained upward. When wars and recessions are discounted, a steady pattern can be seen to have

## The great jobs shake-out

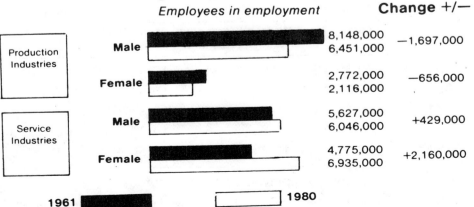

*Employees in employment*

Change +/−

Production Industries

**Male** 8,148,000 6,451,000 −1,697,000

**Female** 2,772,000 2,116,000 −656,000

Service Industries

**Male** 5,627,000 6,046,000 +429,000

**Female** 4,775,000 6,935,000 +2,160,000

1961 1980

started in the 1930s. Around one million extra women have joined Britain's labour force each decade.

As table one shows, the trend has accelerated since the early 1960s. Since 1961, 2.7 million women have joined the labour force, while 500,000 men have left it. (These are net figures: the gross movements of people who join and leave are, of course, far higher.) The combined effect of a declining male labour force and a rising female labour force has been to bring about a market shift in the balance of men and women at work. In 1961, 31 per cent of the labour force consisted of women; the 1980 figure is 40 per cent. Put another way, for every 100 working men in 1961 there were 45 working women. Today, for every 100 working men there are 67 working women.

The greatest change has come among married women. A generation ago, in the early 1950s, barely one married woman in five over the age of 25 worked: today almost three out of five work. (Among unmarried women over 25 the proportion of workers has remained broadly constant at 75 per cent. 'Workers' in this context means all those who define themselves as 'economically active', and includes some people who are unemployed or otherwise available for work.)

The overall changes conceal even greater shifts when different sectors of the economy are considered separately. In the past twenty years 2.4 million jobs have gone in production industries, while 2.6 million new jobs have been created in service industries. This tendency is fairly typical among modern industrialised countries: manufacturing output tends now to grow through investment and modernisation, while it is service industries such as finance, education, health and administration that provide extra jobs. The chart demonstrates how this trend has created more jobs for women and fewer for men. In 1961, most men were employed in production industries — where jobs have declined; on the other hand most women were employed in service industries —

## TABLE 1: MEN AND WOMEN AT WORK
*Figures in millions*

|  | Total labour force | | | | In work | | Unemployed | |
|---|---|---|---|---|---|---|---|---|
|  | Total | Men | Women | Women as % of total | Men | Women | Men | Women |
| 1951 | 22.6 | 15.6 | 7.0 | 31 | 15.4 | 6.9 | 0.2 | 0.1 |
| 1961 | 23.8 | 16.1 | 7.7 | 32 | 15.8 | 7.6 | 0.3 | 0.1 |
| 1971 | 25.1 | 15.9 | 9.2 | 37 | 15.2 | 9.1 | 0.7 | 0.1 |
| 1976 | 25.6 | 15.8 | 9.8 | 38 | 14.8 | 9.5 | 1.0 | 0.3 |
| 1980 (est) | 26.0 | 15.6 | 10.4 | 40 | 14.5 | 9.9 | 1.1 | 0.5 |

'In work' includes self-employed and armed forces.

*SOURCE:* Social Trends 1980 and Department of Employment Gazette.

where job opportunities have expanded.

But that fact alone explains only part of the rise in female employment. In production industries overall, female employment has fallen slightly faster than male employment; but in service industries, 83 per cent of the extra job opportunities since 1961 have been filled by women.

Table two analyses the changes in more detail. More than twice as many women are now employed in finance than 20 years ago; 79 per cent more women work in professional and scientific services (such as teaching and health). And 54 per cent more women work in public administration — central and local government — a sector that has seen almost no growth in male employment.

## TABLE 2: THE JOBS PEOPLE DO
*Employees in employment, in thousands*

|  |  | 1961 | 1971 | 1980 | % change '61–'80 |
|---|---|---|---|---|---|
| Manufacturing | M | 5,730 | 5,546 | 4,730 | −17 |
|  | F | 2,639 | 2,340 | 1,929 | −27 |
| ALL PRODUCTION INDUSTRIES | M | 8,148 | 7,373 | 6,451 | −21 |
|  | F | 2,772 | 2,497 | 2,116 | −24 |
| Communication and distribution | M | 2,778 | 2,487 | 2,385 | −14 |
|  | F | 1,667 | 1,690 | 1,794 | +8 |
| Insurance, banking | M | 377 | 479 | 564 | +50 |
|  | F | 307 | 496 | 639 | +108 |
| Professional, scientific | M | 737 | 1,002 | 1,127 | +53 |
|  | F | 1,387 | 1,987 | 2,476 | +79 |
| Public administration | M | 916 | 996 | 949 | +4 |
|  | F | 395 | 513 | 608 | +54 |
| Misc. services | M | 819 | 893 | 1,022 | +25 |
|  | F | 1,000 | 1,053 | 1,418 | +42 |
| ALL SERVICES | M | 5,627 | 5,858 | 6,046 | +7 |
|  | F | 4,775 | 5,739 | 6,935 | +45 |

*SOURCE:* DE Gazette

**Women and the unions**

The growth of trade union membership among women has been even more striking than the growth in employment. Since 1961, union membership has doubled to four million, as table three shows. Twenty years ago there were four male union members to each female union member; today men outnumber women by barely two-to-one. The reason why female union membership has grown faster than the number of working women is that the *general* growth in unionism has been most marked in the service sector. In a typical service sector, both the *number* of women workers and the *proportion* of women union members has increased by about 50 per cent — so the total number of women union members has more than doubled.

When it comes to unions affiliated to the Trades Union Congress the growth is yet more startling. The figures in table three relate to all unions known to the Government — and not all of these belong to the TUC. But since the early 1960s some large unions with large female memberships have joined the TUC — such as the teachers and the local government officers. In the last twenty years, the number of women members of TUC-affiliated unions has trebled to 3.7 million.

Having said that, there is still some way to go before women become as unionised as men. Between February and July 1980, Market & Opinion Research International conducted a detailed inquiry for the *Sunday Times* on the characteristics of men and women at work and in unions. MORI analysed a total sample of more than 4,000 workers, and more than 2,000 union members. The overall figures tie up closely with known national statistics, although at the edges there are small differences. (Workers in the MORI samples include some who are self-employed; and there are likely to be some people — women especially — who regard themselves as part-time workers but do not show up in government figures.)

## TABLE 3: MEN AND WOMEN IN UNIONS
*Membership of unions in thousands*

|            | Total  | Men   | Women | Women as % of total |
|------------|--------|-------|-------|---------------------|
| 1961       | 9,897  | 7,905 | 1,992 | 20                  |
| 1964       | 10,218 | 8,043 | 2,174 | 21                  |
| 1970       | 11,179 | 8,438 | 2,741 | 25                  |
| 1974       | 11,755 | 8,581 | 3,174 | 27                  |
| 1978       | 13,112 | 9,322 | 3,789 | 29                  |
| 1980 (est) | 13,500 | 9,300 | 4,200 | 31                  |

*SOURCE: DE Gazette; our estimate for 1980*

As table four shows, 28 per cent of women workers in MORI's samples said they belonged to a union, compared with 53 per cent of male workers. The gap narrows a little when only full-time workers are considered, but even here the proportion of women in unions is only two-thirds the proportion of men (36 per cent compared with 53 per cent). But of the three million or so women who work part-time, only 19 per cent belong to unions. (True, MORI found that only 15 per cent of male part-time workers belong to unions; but the total number of such workers is so small that this figure is neither particularly reliable or relevant.)

Among full-time workers, the biggest discrepancies between male and female rates of unionisation occur among 25 to 34 year-olds, among the over 45s, and among manual workers. Indeed, among white-collar workers the difference between male and female unionisation rates is only seven per cent; among blue-collar workers, the difference rises to 24 per cent.

Table five explores the age differences more fully. What emerges with devastating clarity is the impact that bearing and rearing young children has on

## TABLE 4: MEN AND WOMEN IN UNIONS (b)

*Figures show percentage of workers who belong to a union*

|  | Men | Women |
| --- | --- | --- |
| All workers | 53 | 28 |
| Full-time workers | 53 | 36 |
| Part-time workers | 15 | 19 |
| **Full-time workers** | | |
| Aged 18–24 | 42 | 35 |
| 25–34 | 52 | 28 |
| 35–44 | 52 | 42 |
| 45–54 | 63 | 40 |
| 55–64 | 63 | 43 |
| AB (professional, managerial) | 37 | 29 |
| C1 (supervisory, clerical) | 40 | 34 |
| C2 (skilled manual) | 62 | 38 |
| DE (semi- and unskilled manual) | 65 | 42 |

SOURCE: MORI survey for *Sunday Times*
Fieldwork: February–July 1980

working patterns and union membership. A smaller proportion of women aged 25 to 34 work than among any other age group between 18 and 55; a smaller proportion of those who do have a job work full-time than in any other age group; and a smaller proportion of those who work full-time belong to a union than in any other age group. The cumulative result of these biases means that one man in two aged 25 to 34 has a full-time job *and* belongs to a union — *compared with one one woman in 20 in the same age range.*

As a result, the typical male union member in his late thirties or forties has had work and union experience over twenty years; whereas for the typical female union member, work and union experience will be nothing like as continuous. It follows that wherever buggins' turn applies, buggins is seldom a woman.

## Political views of union members

Table six compares some of the general characteristics of men and women in unions. A higher proportion of women union members work part-time than men, a higher proportion vote Conservative, and a higher proportion belong to white-collar households. (Social class here is defined by the job done by the head of the household. Pollsters leave the choice of who that person is to the interviewee; but in practice married women living with a working husband nearly always nominate him rather than themselves.)

It would be wrong to draw the conclusion that union membership has a politically more radicalising effect on men than on women: in general, men are more prone than women to vote Labour. Indeed, the figures in table seven suggest that working class women are more radicalised by union membership than working class men. Male and female members from blue-collar households

## TABLE 5: A WORKING LIFE?

*Figures show percentage of men and women in each age group who . . .*

| Age group | . . . work (full time or part time) | | . . . work full time | | . . . work full time *and* belong to a union | |
|---|---|---|---|---|---|---|
| | M | F | M | F | M | F |
| 18–24 | 87 | 50 | 86 | 39 | 36 | 14 |
| 25–34 | 97 | 43 | 96 | 19 | 51 | 5 |
| 35–44 | 96 | 50 | 95 | 30 | 49 | 13 |
| 45–54 | 91 | 60 | 90 | 30 | 57 | 12 |
| 55–64 | 78 | 34 | 75 | 15 | 47 | 7 |

*SOURCE:* MORI survey for *Sunday Times.*
*Fieldwork: February–July 1980*

have virtually identical political allegiances — they support Labour rather than Conservative by a margin of three-and-a-half to one; in every other demographic group women tend to be more Conservative than men. For example, white-collar male unionists are evenly divided between Labour and Conservative, while white-collar female unionists give the Tories a clear ten per cent lead. (The average national Labour lead at the time of the MORI surveys was five per cent.)

## TABLE 6: HOW DIFFERENT ARE MEN AND WOMEN UNION MEMBERS?

*Figures show percentages of men and women union members who work full-time, part-time, etc.*

|  | Men | Women |
|---|---|---|
| Work full-time | 92 | 65 |
| Work part-time | 1 | 25 |
| Do not work | 8 | 10 |
| **Politics** | | |
| Conservative | 24 | 29 |
| Labour | 59 | 55 |
| Liberal | 13 | 13 |
| **Class** | | |
| AB (managerial, professional) | 13 | 14 |
| C1 (supervisory, clerical) | 16 | 25 |
| Total white collar | 29 | 39 |
| C2 (skilled manual) | 43 | 34 |
| DE (semi- and unskilled manual) | 28 | 27 |
| Total blue-collar | 71 | 61 |

SOURCE: MORI survey for *Sunday Times*
Fieldwork: *February–July 1980*

Table seven also compares the attitudes of men and women in unions to their national union leadership. Both sexes exhibit a similar pattern: blue-collar unionists are slightly more likely to be satisfied than white-collar unionists. The satisfaction figures for men and women are much the same; on the other hand, considerably more male union members are dissatisfied than female members — while women members display a greater degree of uncertainty over whether their union leadership is any good or not.

## Male and female activism

One explanation for the higher number of women 'don't knows' is that union activism is much more a male than a female phenomenon. Twice in recent years MORI has asked union members whether they performed each of a number of activities (see table eight). The areas of male dominance are clear —

## TABLE 7:
## UNION MEMBERS' ATTITUDES TOWARDS POLITICS . . .
*Figures show percentages who support each party*

|  | MALE TU MEMBERS | | | FEMALE TU MEMBERS | | |
|---|---|---|---|---|---|---|
|  | All | white-collar | blue-collar | All | white-collar | blue-collar |
| Conservative | 24 | 39 | 18 | 29 | 46 | 19 |
| Labour | 59 | 39 | 67 | 55 | 36 | 67 |
| Liberal | 13 | 18 | 11 | 13 | 13 | 12 |
| Lab lead | 35 | 0 | 49 | 26 | —10 | 48 |

## . . . AND THEIR OWN UNION
*Figures show answers in percentages to questions: Are you satisfied or dissatisfied with the way your union's national leadership is running your union?*

|  | All | white-collar | blue-collar | All | white-collar | blue-collar |
|---|---|---|---|---|---|---|
| Satisfied | 56 | 53 | 58 | 53 | 49 | 56 |
| Dissatisfied | 33 | 34 | 33 | 22 | 26 | 20 |
| Don't know | 10 | 13 | 9 | 24 | 25 | 24 |
| Satisfied minus dissatisfied | 23 | 19 | 25 | 31 | 26 | 36 |

SOURCE: MORI survey for *Sunday Times*
Fieldwork: April–July 1980

although comparing the 1976 and 1979 results, the gap is slowly narrowing. Men are twice as likely to have gone on strike, three times as likely to have put forward a proposal at a union meeting or served as a shop steward, and four times as likely to have stood on a picket line. On the other hand, as many as 60 per cent of women union members have attended a union meeting, and 40 per cent say they have voted in a union election.

One simple explanation of the male-female differences in union activity is that, as we have seen, men tend to spend considerably more of their lives as union members — so it is intrinsically more likely that at some time they will, for example, go on strike. But that does not explain the whole difference — especially the very small proportion of women who have taken part in what might be termed discretionary activism: i.e., having stood on a picket line, or served as a shop steward or union official. It seems that even allowing for variations in experience, union men are more likely than union women to volunteer for the sharp end of union activity. And it is noticeable that although the proportion of union men who have done none of the things on MORI's list declined between 1976 and 1979, more than one in four union women have a totally inactive record, compared with one in nine men.

## TABLE 8: UNION ACTIVITY
## Q. Have you ever . . .

*Figures show percentage of union members who have performed each activity*

|  | ALL | | MEN | | WOMEN | |
|---|---|---|---|---|---|---|
|  | 1976 | '79 | '76 | '79 | '76 | '79 |
| Been to a union meeting | 75 | 73 | 82 | 78 | 56 | 60 |
| Voted in a union election | 58 | 73 | 82 | 78 | 37 | 40 |
| Gone on strike | 39 | 44 | 46 | 52 | 22 | 24 |
| Put forward a proposal at a union meeting | 30 | 30 | 38 | 37 | 8 | 12 |
| Stood in a picket line | 16 | 15 | 20 | 19 | 6 | 5 |
| Served as a local union official | 14 | 15 | 18 | 18 | 3 | 6 |
| Served as a shop steward | 12 | 13 | 16 | 16 | 2 | 4 |
| None of these | 17 | 16 | 11 | 11 | 33 | 27 |

*SOURCE:* MORI

Fieldwork: October 1976/October 1979

## TABLE 9: PUBLIC ATTITUDES TOWARDS TRADE UNIONS
*Figures show percentages agreeing with each statement*

|  | MEN | | WOMEN | |
| --- | --- | --- | --- | --- |
|  | All | TU members | All | TU members |
| Trade unions are essential to protect workers' interests | 82 | 96 | 62 | 70 |
| The police should have the power to stop mass picketing | 70 | 58 | 80 | 72 |
| Trade unions have too much power in Britain today | 69 | 58 | 75 | 60 |
| The trade union closed shop is a threat to individual liberty | 69 | 56 | 70 | 66 |
| Most trade unions today are controlled by a few extremists | 68 | 55 | 73 | 55 |
| The Labour Party should not be so closely linked to the unions | 55 | 43 | 62 | 54 |
| Bad management is more to blame than the trade unions for Britain's economic problems today | 46 | 57 | 40 | 57 |
| In the long term the government's policies will improve the economy | 44 | 35 | 50 | 41 |
| Trade unions help to improve the efficiency of British industry | 40 | 35 | 50 | 41 |
| Everyone who works should have to belong to a trade union | 24 | 37 | 17 | 32 |

*SOURCE:* MORI survey for *Sunday Times*
Fieldwork: July 1980

Union women also tend to hold more critical attitudes than union men to the powers and responsibilities of trade unions, as table nine shows. The gap is widest on the most crucial issue of all — whether trade unions are essential to protect workers' interests. Almost all union men agree with that statement, but a sizeable 30 per cent of union women either disagree (18 per cent) or aren't sure (12 per cent). Having said that, there are six broad issues on which a majority of both men and women unionists agree. Four of these are critical of general trade union policy: the police, it is felt, should have the power to stop mass picketing; trade unions are thought to have too much power in Britain today; the closed shop is seen as a threat to individual liberty; and most unions are believed to be controlled by extremists. On the other hand, bad management is more widely blamed than are trade unions for Britain's economic problems.

Polling evidence of this nature is sometimes criticised on the left as misleading: do not many interviewees often give snap answers to questions they have not thought much about? And do not even 'moderate' unionists sometimes take militant action when roused by events that threaten their own livelihoods? Both points are fair as far as they go. But the fact remains that the great majority of union members in Britain — both men and women — have not (yet) been convinced by some of the main nostrums of union activists.

Those findings, from MORI's surveys for the *Sunday Times*, concentrate on general political and union issues. They leave open the attitudes of union members to their own jobs and their immediate experience of their own unions where they work. Last summer the *New Statesman* commissioned a further survey from MORI to explore this area.

## Members' views of their own unions

As table ten shows, MORI found that working women are just as likely as working men to consider themselves fairly paid — even though men are, on average, paid 36 per cent more than women. There are many objective explanations of the pay gap — ranging from specific sex discrimination, to the greater opportunities men have to develop continuous careers and build up work experience. The point remains that *subjectively* most women do not feel unfairly treated over pay. Indeed, in MORI's survey, the group that felt most strongly that it was fairly paid consisted of women unionists: 82 per cent agreed their pay was fair.

MORI's results are broadly consistent with the findings of a government survey in 1975, which found slightly higher job satisfaction among women — even low-paid women — than among men. Eighty-eight per cent of women workers interviewed said they were very or fairly satisfied with their jobs, compared with 82 per cent of male workers. (Fuller details of that survey can be found in the 1977 edition of Social Trends.)

One-third of MORI's sample said they would prefer to work shorter hours than have a substantial pay rise, while half disagreed. As with the pay question, there was little difference between the responses of men and women, although women trade unionists were more evenly divided than male union members.

The main difference on this issue involves age rather than sex. Workers under 45 divide 54-31 in favour of having the extra money; among over 45s, the margin is paper-thin — 41 to 39.

A clear difference between male and female attitudes did emerge in response to the proposition that where jobs are scarce, married women should be discouraged from working. Women disagreed by a margin of two-to-one. More men disagree, too; but the margin was a slender eight per cent. As table ten shows, women of all social classes reject the idea by similar margins; but among men there is a clear class difference. A clear majority of white-collar men disagree with the notion of discouraging married women from working, while blue-collar men are evenly split.

To examine why women play a disproportionately small role in unions, MORI tested two hypotheses: that women are more likely to feel that they would

## TABLE 10: WORKERS ATTITUDES TO JOBS AND PAY
### Q. Do you agree or disagree that . . .
*figures in percentages*

| | MEN | | | | WOMEN | | | |
|---|---|---|---|---|---|---|---|---|
| | All | white collar | blue collar | TU memb | All | white collar | blue collar | TU memb |

**On balance I am paid fairly for the work I do.**

| | All | white collar | blue collar | TU memb | All | white collar | blue collar | TU memb |
|---|---|---|---|---|---|---|---|---|
| Agree | 71 | 75 | 69 | 72 | 73 | 72 | 74 | 82 |
| Disagree | 21 | 16 | 21 | 24 | 18 | 24 | 17 | 16 |

**I'd rather work shorter hours than have a substantial pay rise.**

| | All | white collar | blue collar | TU memb | All | white collar | blue collar | TU memb |
|---|---|---|---|---|---|---|---|---|
| | 33 | 29 | 36 | 37 | 34 | 32 | 36 | 44 |
| Disagree | 50 | 51 | 50 | 53 | 47 | 48 | 46 | 49 |

**Where jobs are scarce, married women should be discouraged from working.**

| | All | white collar | blue collar | TU memb | All | white collar | blue collar | TU memb |
|---|---|---|---|---|---|---|---|---|
| Agree | 38 | 33 | 42 | 38 | 28 | 28 | 27 | 28 |
| Disagree | 46 | 51 | 43 | 49 | 56 | 56 | 55 | 59 |

*SOURCE:* MORI survey for *New Statesman*
Fieldwork: August–September 1980

have problems at home if they were more active in their union; and that both men and women prefer male shop stewards. Table eleven shows the results. There is not a great difference between men and women on domestic constraints — but then, as we have seen, trade union women with young children are fairly rare, anyway. In other words, this result reflects in part the fact that women who belong to unions are generally freer of domestic constraints than other women anyway.

As to the issue of whether men make better shop stewards than women, one-third of both men and women agree. More women than men in unions disagree, while more men than women aren't sure — possibly because in some areas where only men work, the question has never arisen.

Finally, MORI asked trade union members in its sample to identify which characteristics, out of a list of ten, applied to their own union. Table twelve shows the results. The most notable finding is that only 11 per cent of union members say their own union is controlled by extremists and militants — a lower figure than any other on the list. This compares with the general belief of 55 per cent of union members that 'most unions today are controlled by a few extremists' (see table nine). It seems that union members think *other* unions are led by extremists, not their own unions.

Male union members seem to feel more in touch than female unionists with what their union is doing, and to feel that the union 'encourages people like me to get involved'. On the other hand, men are twice as likely as women to feel their union is too involved in politics.

## TABLE 11: ATTITUDES TO UNION INVOLVEMENT
### Trade union members
## Q. Do you agree or disagree that . . .
### figures in percentages

|  | All | Men | Women |
| --- | --- | --- | --- |
| **I'd have problems at home if I were more active in the union.** | | | |
| Agree | 27 | 26 | 29 |
| Disagree | 59 | 61 | 55 |
| **Men make better shop stewards than women do.** | | | |
| Agree | 33 | 34 | 32 |
| Disagree | 36 | 33 | 45 |

SOURCE: MORI survey for *New Statesman*
Fieldwork: August–September 1980

Only one-third of women unionists think their union fights hard for equality between men and women; but this seems to reflect the fact that unions are not generally expected to get involved in wider social or family issues. Only 19 per cent of women unionists think their union should do more to meet the needs of workers with young children. There is, though, a vicious circle here. If women with young children are unable to make family arrangements that allow them to work, they are unlikely to be in unions in the first place — so would not show up in any survey of union members. Having said that, there does seem to have been a failure to generate a high degree of feeling among women, let alone men, in unions that such problems matter, and that trade unions have a role to play in solving them.

## TABLE 12: HOW GOOD IS YOUR UNION?
## Q. Which of these applies to your union?
*figures in percentages*

|  | All | Men | Women |
|---|---|---|---|
| Would fight hard to protect my job if it were threatened | 52 | 54 | 48 |
| Tries to keep its members in touch with what the union is doing | 43 | 46 | 32 |
| Good at looking after the interests of people like me | 39 | 39 | 40 |
| Usually holds meetings at times and places that are easy for me to attend | 33 | 34 | 40 |
| Fights hard for equality between men and women at work | 31 | 30 | 33 |
| Union meetings are usually boring | 25 | 27 | 18 |
| Encourages people like me to get involved | 25 | 27 | 19 |
| Too involved in politics and not enough in advancing its members interests | 22 | 25 | 12 |
| Should do more to meet the needs of workers with young children | 16 | 15 | 19 |
| Controlled by extremists and militants | 11 | 12 | 7 |

SOURCE: MORI survey for *New Statesman*
Fieldwork: August–September 1980

Overall, women are just as satisfied as men that their union is 'good at looking after the interests of people like me'. Indeed, despite the critical attitude of most unionists to unions as a whole — as recorded in table nine — most union members seem to have a tolerably favourable impression of their own union. The five *most* widely selected items on MORI's list in table twelve are all positive, while the three *least* widely selected items are all negative. The bogey-image of unions that is sometimes conjured up by Conservative and some right-wing Labour politicians may accord with the general attitudes of union members; but it does not accord with their direct experiences.

# CHAPTER FOUR

# What employers do and say

## ANNA COOTE and PETER KELLNER

A woman can't get equal pay if there isn't a man at her workplace with whom she can claim parity. But how wide-spread is job segregation? How rigid is it? And in what areas of work does it most occur? A study by IFF Research Limited* reveals that male and female workers are separated from each other to a remarkable extent. Forty-five per cent of women work in totally segregated jobs, as do about 75 per cent of men. Less than a third of women are in 'integrated' jobs — defined as those where no more than three-quarters of the people doing the job in one workplace are of the same sex.

The study is based on 764 establishments, each with 11 or more employees, covering all sectors except agriculture, mining, quarrying, construction, public administration and defence. It identifies a range of factors — from working hours to employers' attitudes — which ensure that men continue to enjoy more pay, better conditions and better job opportunities than women. And it thus confirms much of the speculation which has been going on in the past two or three years, as people have sought to explain why the gap between male and female earnings has grown wider, not narrower, despite the new 'equality' laws.

Table one shows how men and women are distributed between well-paid and poorly-paid categories of work. Not only are women concentrated at the bottom of the scale, but they are also excluded entirely from many of the higher-paid jobs. A breakdown of specific non-manual jobs shows that more than three-quarters of employers in the survey hire men exclusively as marketing sales managers, physical scientists and mathematicians, while more than half employ only men as general managers, accountants and technical sales staff. Employ-

* An enquiry into the employment of women, funded jointly by the Equal Opportunities Commission and the SSRC, reported in *Employment Gazette*, Department of Employment, November 1980.

ers admit that women would not be considered (if they applied) for 20 per cent of all jobs currently done by men alone; and that they would have an unequal chance competing for a further 29 per cent of 'men-only' jobs. Table two shows the reasons employers give for not hiring women. They scarcely seem to recognise that they themselves may be partly to blame for women's reluctance to come forward.

Men work longer basic hours, more shifts and more overtime, and all these serve to increase their take-home pay. Forty per cent of women and only 27

## TABLE 1: MEN ARE STILL IN CHARGE
*percentage of workplaces where jobs are filled by . . .*

|  | Men | Women |
| --- | --- | --- |
| Foremen, supervisors | 95 | 5 |
| Skilled manual jobs | 91 | 9 |
| Professional and scientific staff | 89 | 11 |
| Employers, managers | 87 | 13 |
| Intermediate non-manual jobs (e.g. lab technicians) | 56 | 44 |
| Unskilled manual jobs | 55 | 45 |
| Semi-skilled manual jobs | 52 | 48 |
| Junior non-manual jobs (e.g. secretaries, telephonists, shop assistants) | 29 | 71 |
| Personal service (e.g. waiters, hotel staff) | 18 | 82 |

## TABLE 2: WHY EMPLOYERS DON'T HIRE WOMEN
*Where particular jobs were filled only by men in a given establishment, the employer was asked why women were excluded from those jobs. The figures show the answers, as a percentage of employers asked this follow-up question.*

| | |
| --- | --- |
| No women have applied | 43% |
| Women are not strong enough | 27% |
| Union objections | 8% |
| Difficulties over shift working | 6% |

per cent of men work a basic week of 35-39 hours, compared with 48 per cent of women and 65 per cent of men who put in between 44 and 48 basic hours. IFF's Andrew McIntosh points out that the Factory Acts (which bar women from night work, some shift systems and long hours of overtime) regularly affect only 21 per cent of jobs in the survey. He therefore concludes: 'It does not appear that shift working is a major obstacle to women's employment opportunities, nor that it has a great effect on differential earnings between men and women.'

Overtime, on the other hand, makes a big difference (with almost twice as many men as women engaged in it), so does the preponderance of part-timers in the female workforce. In six years, the proportion of employers who have female part-timers in their workforce has risen from 79 to 88 per cent. The study shows that more than four-fifths of part-time women get the same rates as full-timers. But they lose out badly over sick pay and pensions. Though more than 70 per cent of employers offer sick pay and pension schemes which go beyond the provisions of the state, part-timers are eligible for only 14 per cent of these pension schemes, and for 30 per cent of the sick pay arrangements.

Methods of recruitment and training leave women at a disadvantage, too. As the authors explain, discrimination against women in formal methods of recruitment — such as job advertising and employment agencies — is now pro-

## TABLE 3: HOW BIASED ARE THE BOSSES?
### Employers' perceptions of how well men and women perform at work
*figures show percentage of all employers surveyed*

|  | Men better than women | | | Women better than men | | |
|---|---|---|---|---|---|---|
|  | 1973 | 1979 | change | 1973 | 1979 | change |
| Not taking days off for sickness | 53 | 42 | —11 | 5 | 6 | + 1 |
| Not taking days off for other reasons | 47 | 69 | +22 | 10 | 2 | — 8 |
| Staying with one firm | 44 | 18 | —26 | 15 | 23 | + 8 |
| Being punctual | 31 | 19 | —12 | 15 | 12 | — 3 |
| Working safely | 22 | 5 | —17 | 24 | 11 | —13 |
| Carrying out instructions | 13 | 2 | —11 | 18 | 12 | — 6 |
| Working hard | 12 | 3 | — 9 | 16 | 12 | — 4 |
| Working conscientiously | 11 | 4 | — 7 | 26 | 14 | —12 |

hibited by law. However, informal methods, involving contact with employees (who are likely to be male, especially in the case of higher-paid jobs) tend to fall outside the scope of legislation — and it is here that sex discrimination can easily occur. Sixty-six per cent of women and 44 per cent of men are recruited by formal methods, compared with 21 per cent of women and 36 per cent of men by informal methods.

Equal numbers of women and men take advantage of on-the-job training, but men get far more off-site and off-the-job training (17 per cent, compared with seven per cent of women), which tends to be more expensive, as well as more significant as a means to promotion.

Employers show an alarming degree of complacency in this area. Half of them claim there has never been any discrimination in their establishment, and 27 per cent insist there is no need for change. They have modified their perceptions about male and female performance at work and now claim there are fewer differences between the sexes. The main exception, as Table three shows, concerns taking days off work for reasons other than sickness. The General

## TABLE 4: WHY WOMEN DON'T REACH THE TOP
**Employers' views of why few women rise to senior positins or do skilled work**

*Figures show percentage of all employers surveyed*

|  | 1973 | 1979 | change |
|---|---|---|---|
| **Reasons relating to women themselves:** | | | |
| Not career conscious | 37 | 39 | + 2 |
| Break in working life | 23 | 14 | — 9 |
| Change jobs too often; unreliable | 20 | 2 | —18 |
| Family ties; unwilling/unable to take responsibility | 16 | 26 | +10 |
| Others | 22 | 6 | —16 |
| **Other resons:** | | | |
| Male prejudice/management discrimination | 21 | 7 | —14 |
| Attitude of society/tradition | 15 | 24 | + 9 |
| Less chance to train | 15 | 6 | — 9 |
| Others | 6 | 5 | — 1 |

Household Survey (HMSO, 1977) has confirmed that women do *not* take more days off work than men — for sickness or any other reason — so it would appear that the employers' view may spring from prejudice rather than from fact.

The number of employers who believe more women should occupy senior jobs had declined slightly in six years (from 46 to 44 per cent), although more now think women should have training for skilled jobs. Fewer of them now believe there is anything they or the government can do to promote equality any further. And in general, employers are still very ready with explanations for under-achievement which reflect on the women themselves.

# TUC Charter:
# Equality for women within trade unions

*Commended by the General Council of the Trades Union Congress 'to all union executives and committees . . . for the integration of women within trade unions at all levels'. Endorsed by Congress, 1979.*

1 The National Executive Committee of the union should publicly declare to all its members the commitment of the union to involving women members in the activities of the union at all levels.

2 The structure of the union should be examined to see whether it prevents women from reaching the decision-making bodies.

3 Where there are large women's memberships but no women on the decision-making bodies special provision should be made to ensure that women's views are represented, either through the creation of additional seats or by co-option.

4 The National Executive Committee of each union should consider the desirability of setting up advisory committees within its constitutional machinery to ensure that the special interests of its women members are protected.

5 Similar committees at regional, divisional, and district level could also assist by encouraging the active involvement of women in the general activities of the union.

6 Efforts should be made to include in collective agreements provision for time off without loss of pay to attend branch meetings during working hours where that is practicable.

7 Where it is not practicable to hold meetings during working hours every effort should be made to provide child-care facilities for use by either parent.

8   Child-care facilities, for use by either parent, should be provided at all district, divisional and regional meetings and particularly at the union's annual conference, and for training courses organised by the union.

9   Although it may be open to any members of either sex to go to union training courses, special encouragement should be given to women to attend.

10  The content of journals and other union publications should be presented in non-sexist terms.

# A study of trade union branches in the Hull area

## JANE STAGEMAN

*It is beyond the scope of this booklet to reproduce the study in full. It can be obtained, price £1, from the Industrial Studies Unit, Adult Education Department, University of Hull. We include here a brief summary of the project and questionnaire results, together with the final chapter (with minor amendments) in which the author presents her conclusions*

## The project

With a research grant from the Equal Opportunities Commission, Jane Stageman made a study of women members in five trade union branches in the Hull area. The branches were selected to span blue-collar and white-collar jobs, as well as centralised and dispersed workplaces. They were:

1. A 'water services' branch of NALGO (National Association of Local Government Officers), which drew its membership from clerical, administrative, professional and technical staffs in a division of the Yorkshire Water Authority.
2. A 'health services' branch of NALGO, with members among white-collar employees in 12 hospitals in the Beverley District, 16 hospitals and a health centre in the Hull District and a number of community clinics in both.
3. A 'health services' branch of NUPE (National Union of Public Employees), covering three hospitals, a maternity home and a number of clinics.
4. A 'shop workers' branch of USDAW (Union of Shop, Distributive & Allied Workers), covering workers in Co-operative Stores, slaughter houses, wholesale and retail distribution.
5. A 'manufacturing branch' of USDAW, based in a dairy products factory.

Female shop stewards were interviewed to establish the length, type and degree of their involvement, and to identify the problems encountered not only by the stewards but also by their women members, when it came to participating in union affairs. Questionnaires were distributed, 108 of them were completed and returned [1]. These probed women members' views on the issues on which they felt their union should be active, both generally and in relation to women. A section was included to identify barriers to participation. The questionnaire also sought to collect biographical and work data, and record the current participation of the women union members. Branch meetings were observed and interviews were conducted with full-time and branch officials of the unions concerned.

An attempt was made to establish how union activists differed from non-activists, in their age, marital status, home responsibilities, education and occupation. It was found, in the main, that women who indicated they had sought or held a union position were older, had a greater proportion of their children over 18; were likely to have a father who was in a union; had a father and/or husband who was active in their own union; were more likely to be working full-time; had been in their job longer and felt more consistently that they needed to work for money for necessities.

The table opposite shows which 'personal' and 'union-related' factors the respondents to the questionnaire believed would encourage participation in union activities.

## CONCLUSION: THE PROBLEMS AND THE ALTERNATIVES

### Obstacles of a practical nature

It is perhaps not surprising that obstacles of a practical nature were particularly stressed by women in the sample who were currently attempting to combine work and family responsibilities. The responsibility for rearing children and for housework has generally shown little change in recent years even in families with wage earning wives. The full extent to which women in this position experience practical difficulties to union participation will depend however, on the availability and access to other agencies in taking over the functions associated with being a wife and mother. Whether experienced to a greater or lesser extent by their women members in this position, the unions in the study all presented a number of practical obstacles at branch level. All the branches held their monthly or annual union membership meetings in evening hours when women are expected to carry out their household duties. Admittedly, there had been experiments of holding meetings during lunch time hours at work-places in two branches but these had met with limited success due to their inability to overcome other effects of women's extra responsibilities, such as doing the family shopping. In all but one branch, the evening meetings were also held away from the workplace. A different location could complicate further the attendance of women who want to be accessible to meet family emergencies and have chosen their place of work for precisely this reason. Women's inability to participate in branch meetings in one union, USDAW, theoretically held further penalties for their union involvement. According to the rule book, 50 per cent attendance was needed in any year to be able to stand for union office at the Annual General Meeting. Indeed, women with home and family responsibilities, who were prepared to take on office at branch level, encounter-

**Factors which 108 female respondents from the five union branches believed would encourage participation in union activities.**

| PERSONAL | No. | % | UNION | No. | % |
|---|---|---|---|---|---|
| Fewer home responsibilities | 51 | 55 | Meetings held in more convenient places | 34 | 37 |
| Giving up other activities | 15 | 16 | Meetings held at a different time | 11 | 12 |
| Feeling more confident | 41 | 44 | Meetings held in work time | 59 | 64 |
| Going to meetings with someone I know | 34 | 37 | Make union matters easier to understand | 57 | 62 |
| My husband agreeing to me being active in the union | 11 | 12 | Provide childcare facilities so I could come to meetings | 5 | 5 |
| Knowing that women can be as competent as men in union affairs | 37 | 40 | Make more information available about how unions work | 52 | 56 |
| Male union members giving me a chance to air my views | 25 | 27 | Organise more social events | 14 | 15 |
| Having a greater interest in union affairs | 52 | 56 | Running education courses | 22 | 24 |
| Nothing would make it easier | 10 | 11 | Creating opportunities so women could get together and discuss matters of interest to them | 43 | 46 |
| Other | 4 | 4 | Other | 3 | 3 |

# The Fawcett Society

*Campaigners for equality between the sexes since 1866*

Parnell House (Fifth Floor), 25 Wilton Road, London SW1V 1LW
Telephone: 01-828 1981

| President of Society: | Presides at Executive: | General Secretary: |
|---|---|---|
| Baroness Seear | Mary Stott OBE | Catherine Dennis MA |

## THE FAWCETT SOCIETY

● is the direct heir of the constitutional suffrage societies which under Dame Millicent Garrett Fawcett's leadership worked unceasingly for votes for women on equal terms with men from 1866 to 1928.

● has campaigned throughout its long history to influence Parliament and to educate public opinion to accept equal status for women, equal citizenship rights, equal responsibilities in the home and in public life, equal educational and job opportunities and equal pay for work of equal value.

● works energetically today for the economic and social indepence of all women, whether married or single, especially through revision of our tax and pension laws and extension of supportive child care; for adequate representation of women in Parliament, on all public bodies and in the Media; and against all discrimination based on sex, whether in law, practice or custom.

● holds regular open meetings and occasional seminars on subjects of importance to women, especially in the fields of education and employment.

● works through sub-committees from members with special interest and expert knowledge of Public Affairs, International Affairs, Education and Employment. These sub-committees, which meet regularly, monitor and react to current developments, undertake research and make representations to Ministers and Government departments.

● co-operates actively with other organisations who share our aims.

**The Fawcett Library** is now in the City of London Polytechnic, Old Castle Street, E1 (near Aldgate East underground). It is Britain's main historical resource on women. Tel: 01-283 1030 ext. 570. Hours: Mon 1pm–8.30pm; Tue–Fri 10am–5pm.

**SUBSCRIPTIONS:** Fawcett Society: £6 per year with an option to full-time students and retired members of paying £3 per year. Fawcett Library: £2.50 per year for Fawcett Society members (£5 a year for others).

Applications from General Secretary at address above.

ed further problems in all the unions. Branch committees (which are encouraged in every rule book) again held their meetings either wholly or partly outside worktime. Even straight after work is difficult for women who are expected to cook the tea. Moreover, this was likely to affect willingness not only to hold branch office but also to become shop steward in the branches where active shop stewards doubled as committee members.

Education and training for shop steward responsibilities also presented practical problems in the branches of NALGO and USDAW. These branches did not, at the time of study, systematically encourage the use of day release facilities or in-plant training for this purpose. It was significant therefore, that it was only in these branches that women were found who, although offered, had been unable to finish or take up the facility of union education because it involved time outside working hours.

Some union activities however, were generally carried out in worktime in all the branches. These were matters directly concerned with handling members' grievances and related to negotiating activities. Unfortunately, as the main negotiating activities in all the branches were predominantly done by men, they had the greater advantage of this facility. Indeed, in general, there was a considerable variation in the provision and use of facilities by the women within and between branches, and a general lack of knowledge about the extent of their rights in this area. [2] A lack of clarity over these issues may well have acted as another disincentive to women wanting to combine shop steward activity with home and family responsibilities.

The sample suggested that women working part-time were under-represented in shop steward positions. Yet part-time workers, who often choose these hours because of home and family responsibilities, probably suffer the most exploited conditions in the labour market. However, none of the branches demonstrated any particular efforts in their arrangements to meet the practical needs of such women, for example by adjusting hours of education and training courses or making payments to cover hours spent outside work attending courses, meetings and servicing members. It seems generally true that all unions are happy to exploit these workers in a similar way to employers.

This range of obstacles to women with home and family responsibilities helps to explain why the majority of women holding positions in the branches in the study had relinquished the main load of their family responsibilities (the majority of their children were over eighteen). It also helps explain why divorced, separated and widowed women appeared to be over-represented in the sample. It is clearly significant too, that the handful of women who had been able to get involved in union activities at a divisional or national level, were all single, childless or with children well into their teenage years. In other words, these women had rid themselves of the practical aspects ensuing from the sexual division of labour encouraged in our society.

## Obstacles of an institutional nature

The second group of obstacles to union participation which were highlighted by women in the sample were those of a more strictly institutional nature. A considerable number of women stressed that they experienced a lack of confidence and interest in union participation and knowledge and understanding of the operations of the union. The fact that these feelings were expressed is not surprising, since women are still being encouraged in our society to assume primarily a domestic identity and not to develop their potential fully in other areas of their lives. Women members who were single and childless in the study sample particularly felt obstacles of an institutional nature to their union participation. This may well reflect the ideological repercussions of not fitting into the socially accepted role of wife and mother. The familiarity of unionisation in differing occupations and economic classes must also be taken into account when assessing the differing responses from non-manual compared to manual women in this area. Generally however, the full extent to which women experience institutional obstacles to their union participation will depend on a variety of factors including the influences of family, friends, education, their work situation and activities in other organisations.

By their very location in the 'male' sphere of work, all the union branches presented an institutional obstacle of some degree to their women members. As one woman wrote:

Most young women find themselves having very little time for outside activities when they have young families to see to, and by the time they are of an age when they could spare the time it is not uncommon for them to have developed a great lack of self confidence through their lives being devoted to domestic problems to suddenly get up at a union meeting and voice their own opinions. Television coverage at union gatherings hardly enhances the picture, where some people become so belligerent that I doubt any woman would dare to participate.

All of the union branches went on to augment this fundamental obstacle in more particular ways. The acquisition of greater knowledge and understanding of union matters was made more difficult in two branches of two unions, NALGO and USDAW, by their inability to provide basic information and servicing for members. The USDAW 'shopworkers' branch drew its members from a variety of shops spread widely across Hull and its outskirts. Servicing and information differed dramatically due to the limited shop steward coverage available over such a big area. In two workplaces, smaller units had arisen spontaneously to deal more effectively with the problems and needs of members. However, because of their spontaneous method of growth these units lacked the beneficial links with other workplaces and the rest of the union structure. Similar to the USDAW branch, the NALGO 'health' branch drew its members from a variety of workplaces spread over an ever greater geographical area, making good membership communication difficult. NUPE, organising in a similar industrial situation to this NALGO branch, had reduced the problem to some extent by basing its organisational unit on a smaller area. This was in line with the national recommendations of the union, which advocate a branch move towards the smallest functional units while maintaining permanent links in committee form in line with management levels in most of the employment fields in which it organises. Such a move, ensuring that links with workplaces and the union structure are maintained, is one way of providing a manageable number and location of members to which adequate information and servicing can be supplied. Indeed, it was only in the branch which possessed these characteristics (small and concentrated membership), that any special arrangements had been made to service new membership and to provide a means of communicating to members locally in the form of a newsletter. In general, the basic explanation of union aims and operations was overlooked by branch practices in the sample. This was particularly true in branches which did not have to maintain membership by active recruitment, i.e. closed shops. However, shop stewards who experienced problems with knowledge and understanding of their own union structure were to be found in every branch. The general lack of expectancy of women's union participation and, in many cases, their employment in traditionally weak and relatively new areas of unionisation, makes this basic explanation of union aims and operations fundamental to encouraging their involvement. If this opportunity is not produced during working hours, then the practical obstacles which many women have in addition will mean there is no avenue open for them to fill this gap. One woman clearly showed in her response how a lack of proper knowledge and understanding of union practices perpetuated the likelihood that women would form ideological obstacles to their own participation:

> The general impression I have of unions is not one of amicable people getting together to try and improve life in general for everyone — but more of politically minded radicals who take the opportunity of voicing their views at all times. To get women interested in union activities they would have to present a new image — with more inside information on exactly what the meetings are about being given greater publicity.

The lack of skills as well as information provide obstacles to participation and here again the union branches demonstrated practices of a problematic nature. Although allowed for in the rule books and paid lip service to in the Annual General Meeting, turnover of lay representatives was generally not experienced in any of the branches. In one branch, shop steward turnover was explicitly stated as 'bad' and in another, the ideals of 'continuity' and 'experience' were proudly adhered to. Clearly, if tasks are rotated too frequently an individual does not have time to learn the job well and acquire a sense of satisfaction. On the other hand, if a job is held too long by one person, formally or informally, it often becomes seen as that person's property and can become difficult to relinquish or control. The major problem for women in this situation is that the majority of positions in the trade union movement have traditionally been held by men. Proportionately more men held the post of shop steward in all the branches in the study. In all but one branch moreover, they also held the positions which are generally considered most important in the branch, i.e. branch secretary and union negotiators. It is easy to see how, if the principles of continuity and experience are explicitly or implicitly adhered to, women will find it extremely difficult to gain these skills. It is clearly significant that the women who were currently shop stewards emphasised the influence of the family, not the union, in gaining confidence and knowledge to take on this particular responsibility. Therefore, the exceptional opportunity to gain these basic skills and information in a situation where women are expected to do so and accepted (i.e. in the family), provided the link and confidence needed to encourage them to take on the responsibility in their union branches. In some cases this was also encouraged by personal injustice at work or the support of other women workers. It is also notable that the majority of women who had sought or were holding a union position had the virtues of age and work experience to aid their credibility.

## Obstacles of male domination

Women who were most likely to be experiencing obstacles to union participation at a practical as well as an ideological level, were most strongly represented in the responses suggesting that their union branches were 'a man's world'. These were married women, women with children and women at the manual end of the job market. It was left however, to women who were divorced, separated, or widowed, most explicitly to state the obstacle of male dominance. This could be because these women are no longer in the contradictory position of attempting to live and share a life with one man while acknowledging that men contribute to the oppressed situation of women in all areas of society. This male dominance, explicitly or implicitly recognised by the women members in the sample, has its roots in the patriarchal system operating at economic, ideological and repressive levels in our society. The way in which women experience the influence of patriarchy varies primarily by economic class, race and sexuality.

The union branches all perpetuated this societal experience of their women members. Men held proportionately more shop steward positions in every branch and in all but one, the positions with access to most resources and power. In consequence the union structure replicated the hierarchical positioning of the sexes found in employment and all other areas of society. It is no doubt significant that the only woman who reached the position of branch secretary was fairly high up in the employment structure at her workplace.

Sexist behaviour, although difficult to quantify, was seen at most branch meetings during observation. It was demonstrated most explicitly in the meeting of the USDAW manufacturing branch when male members left the room as soon as the women brought up an issue of particular relevance to their employment position. Differing ratios of male/female membership clearly made no impression on the dominance of male interests in union activities and issues.

The fact that the interests of men and women were generally different in every branch was ensured by the sexual division of labour operating in both the public and private sectors of employment where the unions were organising. There was no evidence however, of action being taken in any of the branches to attempt to erode these occupational divisions between the sexes, despite the fact that women members showed most concern over this aspect of their employment position. Women members in only two branches expressed a definite desire for union action on other aspects of their position in society which condition and perpetuate their employment experience. This desire however, showed a stronger relation to their wage and employment position than to an awareness stimulated through branch discussion and action. Indeed, in none of the branches had any efforts been made to provide an opportunity for membership to discuss union policy, or the policy of the trade union movement generally, on women's position in society. Moreover, no branch had conducted a coherent examination of the ways in which the branch organisation and structure could be adapted to meet the needs of female membership and to ensure that female members were assured of an equally representative position in the structure.

Male dominance, preventing women's power representation in the branch structure and preventing a proper satisfaction of their needs, could explain why so many women members in the sample appeared to lack interest in participating in their union. In other words, union activity appears to require not only a stripping of some of the practical and ideological consequences of being a woman but also to require motivations and interests similar to those of men.

## The alternatives

The changing of women into 'honorary' men is one option available in attempting to encourage women's trade union involvement. The other, which I believe in the long term is likely to be more effective and valuable for women, and indeed the trade union movement as a whole, is the changing of trade unions to meet the needs of their women members. Unfortunately, the main emphasis of the effective policy of the trade union movement towards women has generally been concentrated on the first option. It is true that the TUC, under pressure from women inside and outside the movement, has gradually accepted an ever-widening list of aims to end discriminations against women in society. However, these have been treated as 'special interest' grievances and have failed, generally, to be pursued as part of the main policy interests of the movement and seen as an integral part of negotiating objectives. Moreover, the passing of egalitarian resolutions at conference level, seems to have made no impact on the continuance of oppressive activities by male trade unionists towards their own wives and daughters in their own homes. The uncritical acceptance of this contradiction has served to perpetuate the present state of affairs — in which greater opportunities for women to develop their potential are still enjoyed by relatively few. Therefore, it is still 'a certain type of woman' [3] who can pursue active involvement in their trade union. This also remains true because of the reluctance, on the part of most sections of the trade union movement, to recognise that the structure of their organisation is also an agent of the oppression which women endure.

The General Council of the TUC recently commended a Charter to all union executives and committees (see Appendix 1). This Charter aims to fill 'the need to give women fuller equality within the individual unions and, just as important, to encourage women to take full advantage of existing and new opportunities open to them within their trade unions'. Is this again a token response to a special interest grievance? Or is this a real sign that an effort is being made to come to grips with such obstacles to trade union participation as are highlighted by the women in the Hull sample?

Certainly, some obstacles of a practical nature are given recognition in this new charter. Point six suggests:

> Efforts should be made to include in collective agreements provision for time off without loss of pay to attend branch meetings during working hours where that is practicable.

The importance of this provision to many women in the Hull sample, particularly those with the extra burden of home and family responsibilities, suggests that unions concerned to encourage more women to participate should not be making 'efforts' to obtain this provision but should be giving it a *priority* in their negotiations. Indeed, ideally they should be pursuing this provision for every meeting connected with trade union affairs [4]. However, the inclusion of the phrase, 'where that is practicable' makes it seem unlikely that branches with large and geographically spread membership will even consider adopting these minimum demands. It is clearly easier for branches to say that it is 'impracticable', than it is to act to re-organise their structure to *make* it practicable. Yet, the importance of this provision for the majority of women is undeniable. It is of little use to have, for example, a discussion on the policies of injustice, when the meeting which decides how they should be implemented is so timed or placed that those to whom the injustice is done cannot attend. Equally, it is of limited use to make a gesture of recognition towards one aspect of women's position (i.e. the provision of childcare facilities at meetings in points seven and eight of the Charter), while providing no evidence of a thorough-going commitment to change this position at a general level. This approach can only add to the worries of the mother who is caught in the contradiction of being encouraged by society, on the one hand, to show commitment and care for her child, and by trade unions, on the other, freely to relinquish this responsibility to unknown hands, at the occasional union meeting. It is also not only at meeting times that women, who want to participate equally in trade union affairs, are going to need relieving of childcare responsibilities. Women working part-time, for example, may need an afternoon service in order to attend union education and training courses. Clearly, if this recognition of childcare responsibilities is not going to remain token, it must be accompanied by a campaign aimed at ensuring that the responsibility can be freely and conveniently shared through the provision of facilities by the state, employers, trade unions and within the family and community setting.

The particular position of part-time workers, who are predominantly women, is not mentioned in the TUC Charter for Equality Within the Trade

Unions. Yet this Hull study suggests that it is these women who are particularly exploited when participating in trade union affairs. In order to encourage more women in this position to become active in their union it is imperative that the advantages that full-time workers enjoy through legislation [5] are also extended to them. In the area of education and training it is particularly important that unions give consideration to the running of part-time day release courses or ensure that any extra hours spent on a full day course are compensated in a similar manner to full-time workers. Indeed, it is important for all women with home and family responsibilities to have the opportunity to attend union education and training on a day release basis and at a place which is accessible from their homes. At the present time, it is only with this type of provision that women with home and family responsibilities can be expected to benefit equally from the availability of such facilities. It is to be hoped that unions will interpret this as one aspect of the 'special encouragement' that the TUC advocate in the ninth point of their Charter. This point deals with the educational and training needs of women trade unionists:

> Although it may be open to any members of either sex to go to union training courses, special encouragement should be given to women to attend. [6]

Even if we assume that women enjoy the practical facilities freely to attend meetings and courses there are, as suggested by the women in the Hull study, the institutional obstacles and the obstacles of male dominance to be overcome. As well as the ninth point, the Charter makes two other types of 'special' provision in this area. Points four and five suggest the setting up of advisory committees in order that, 'the special interests of its women members are protected'. Point four suggests that the desirability of these should be considered at a national level and point five, at regional, divisional and district level. The danger of setting up such advisory committees is that they can easily be seen as accepting the responsibility for solving the obstacles that women face in trade union participation, and so absolving the rest of the union from fulfilling its obligations. One remedy for this lies in ensuring that women on such committees have representation on decision taking bodies at *all* levels in the union. This could be achieved by the implementation of the other 'special' provision in point three of the Charter:

> Where there are large women's memberships but no women on the decision-making bodies special provision should be made to ensure that women's views are represented either through the creation of additional seats or by co-option. [7]

The women on these decision-making bodies could then raise set issues within the union for action by all members, male and female. One major problem with this approach is that it assumes that women who take up such positions are numerically strong and confident enough to ensure that they do not become overruled by male views and interests. The Hull study suggests that education and training courses could play an important role in this area. This is through building up women's confidence and skills to feel strong enough to pursue union issues of importance to women generally. However, a second problem with this approach is its acceptance of the hierarchical nature of trade union organisation and its encouragement of leaders, which will lead ultimately to the concentration of information, skills and decision-making in the hands of relatively few women in each union. This need for hierarchical structuring has been strongly challenged by the movement which, in the last decade, has been most successful in encouraging activity and a collective consciousness and solidarity amongst women. Women in this movement, the women's liberation movement (WLM) have stated:

> Since it [the WLM] challenges one of the most fundamental power-structures, power based on sex, it has consciously sought to be non-authoritarian, believing women can work and campaign together by co-operation, without the need for arbitrary rules and officials. [8]

An understanding of women's general lack of confidence has been moulded into this movement from its very inception. The basic form of organisation is based on the small group which gives the opportunity for women to come together to share their experiences and feelings of oppression and through the understanding of the similarity of their situation they find a common ground for action. The success of this form of organisation in the women's movement suggests there is a strong case for developing similar opportunities for groups of women to get together in trade unions. This could happen at grass-roots level, in branches, and also at larger meetings of women on a regional and national basis. In this way the views and feelings of as many women as possible could be discovered and they could become actively included in the fight on everyday issues and in the choosing of priority areas for action. An involvement of women in this way would also alleviate the danger of advisory committees, and women in seats on decision making bodies, taking issues away from the day-to-day action of women on the shop floor. I believe it is the women at such gatherings that should be responsible for deciding how point two of the charter should be carried out in every union:

> The structure of the union should be examined to see whether it prevents women from reaching the decision-making bodies.

This would actively incorporate as many women as possible in the process of forming new structures and procedures which would meet not only the demands of men but also the demands of women. I believe this is necessary if any union is really going to fulfill the first point of the charter:

> . . . the commitment of the union to involving women members in the activities at all levels.

The fulfillment of this aim is not only likely to win active support for the trade union movement by the majority of women workers, but would also incorporate the valuable lesson that has been learnt by those women in the women's liberation movement. This is the recognition that control and exploitation in what is generally considered as one's 'personal' life, in love, friendship, sexual relations, children etc., are as politically important as the control and exploitation experienced in more 'public' spheres, such as waged work. Indeed, as has been argued throughout this study, the experience of control and exploitation in both areas is inextricably linked. If the trade union movement could incorporate this valuable lesson into its aims and objectives, as well as its structure and organisation, I believe it will also have found a means of moving beyond its confinement to basic economic demands, which has so severely hindered its political development.

1. Originally, 300 questionnaires were distributed, in statistically comparable proportions, to six branches, i.e. the five mentioned here and a sixth, a 'manufacturing' branch of the Transport & General Workers' Union. The latter was unable to distribute the questionnaire to its members, due to workplace pressures. However, interviews conducted with members of the branch, and observations of its meetings, are a part of the study and have contributed towards the conclusions. The other five branches distributed a total of 210 questionnaires to their members.

2. This was also found in research done by Fryer, B., Fairclough, A.A., Manson, T.B., 'Facilities for Female Shop Stewards. The Employment Protection Act and Collective Agreements' in the *British Journal of Industrial Relations*, Vol. 16, 1978 pp. 160-174.

3. This phrase was used by a male union official in the study when discussing the competence of women in trade union affairs.

4. At present there is provision in legislation, *Employment Protection (Consolidation) Act 1978*, S.28, for members to take time-off in work time to participate in trade union activities. This provision, however, does not include payment.

5. At present there is provision in legislation, *Employment Protection (Consolidation) Act 1978*, S.27, for shop stewards working over sixteen hours to have time off, with pay, for carrying out their duties and attending related education and training courses.

6. S.48(2) of the 1975 *Sex Discrimination Act* allows special provision to be made to open training opportunities to women only where there has been no women, or comparatively few women, holding a post in the last twelve months.

7. S.49(1) of the 1975 *Sex Discrimination Act* allows special provision to be made by unions where it is considered that women's representation on decision making committees does not reflect their membership. However, where additional seats are created for women and they are filled by election — rather than by co-option — participation in such elections cannot be restricted to women.

8. Women's Research and Resources Centre, The Women's Information, Referral and Enquiry Service (WIRES) and A Woman's Place, *Women's Liberation: An Introduction*, Women in Print, December, 1977, p.1.

# Extended bibliography on women workers and trade unions

Allen, V.L. *The Sociology of Industrial Relations*, London; Longman, 1971

Amsden, A.H. *The Economics of Women and Work*, London; Penguin, 1980

Bain, G.S. *The Growth of White Collar Unionism*, London; Oxford University Press, 1970

Bain, G.S. and Price, R. 'Union Growth Revisited: 1948-1974 in Perspective' in *British Journal of Industrial Relations*, Vol. 14, 1976

Barker, D.L. and Allen, S. (ed.) *Dependence and Exploitation in Work and Marriage*, London; Longman, 1976

Barker, D.L. and Allen, S. (ed.) *Sexual Divisions and Society: Process and Change*, London; Tavistock, 1976

Batstone, E., Boraston, I. and Frenkel, S. *Shop Stewards in Action*, Oxford; Blackwell, 1977

Baxandell, R. 'Women in American Trade Unions: an historical analysis' in *The Rights and Wrongs of Women*, (ed.) Mitchell, J. and Oakley, A., Harmondsworth; Penguin, 1976

Beechey, V. 'Some Notes on Female Wage Labour in Capitalist Production' in *Capital and Class*, Conference of Socialist Economists, No. 3, Autumn, 1977

Beynon, H. *Working for Ford*, Wakefield; E.P., 1975

Blackburn, R.M. *Union Character and Social Class*, London; Batsford, 1976

Blaxall, M. and Reagen, B. *Women and the Workplace: the Implications of Occupational Segregation*, Chicago; University of Chicago, 1967

Boraston, I., Clegg, H.A. and Rimmer, M. *Workplace and Union*, Oxford; Blackwell, 1975

Boston, S. *Women Workers and the Trade Unions*, London; Davis-Poynter, 1980

Braverman, H. *Labor and Monopoly Capital*, New York; Monthly Review Press, 1974

Brown, W.A. *Piecework Bargaining*, Oxford; Blackwell, 1973

# Women's Rights Publications from NCCL

NCCL's Rights for Women Unit's latest publication is this pack containing a series of information sheets and discussion notes covering eight subjects of crucial importance in the struggle for women's rights.

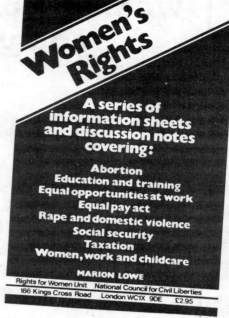

A series of information sheets and discussion notes covering:

Abortion
Education and training
Equal opportunities at work
Equal pay act
Rape and domestic violence
Social security
Taxation
Women, work and childcare

MARION LOWE

Rights for Women Unit   National Council for Civil Liberties
186 Kings Cross Road    London WC1X  9DE      £2.95

The subjects covered are:

- Abortion
- Education and training
- Equal Opportunities at work
- Equal Pay Act
- Rape and domestic violence
- Social security
- Taxation
- Women, work and childcare

**Each note is in A4 format, and the series is collected in a special folder.**

**COMPILED BY
Marion Lowe**

**Shift Work Swindle**
*Jean Coussins*. The arguments against the repeal of protective legislation for women in factories.
*NCCL 1979*                45p

**Income Tax and Sex Discrimination**
*Patricia Hewitt*. A practical guide to income tax highlighting the injustices which still face women.
*NCCL 1979*                75p

**Part-time Workers Need Full-time Rights**
*Ann Sedley*. All the rights of part-time workers, and how NCCL thinks the law should change.
*NCCL 1980*                75p

**The Unequal Breadwinner**
*Ruth Lister* and *Leo Wilson*. How women are penalised when they are the main breadwinners in their families.

All prices include postage and packing. Please send correct remittance with your order.

**NCCL Rights for Women Unit**

**National Council for Civil Liberties**
186 Kings Cross Road, London WC1X 9DE

Brown, W.A., Ebsworth, R. and Terry, M. *Factors Affecting Shop Steward Organisation in Britain*, Warwick University, Mimeo, 1977

Buxton, N.K. and Mackay, I.D. *British Employment Statistics: Guide to Sources and Methods*, Oxford; Blackwell, 1978

Campbell, B. 'United We Fall' in *Red Rag*, London, September 1980

Campbell, B. and Charlton, V. 'Work to Rule — Wages and the Family' in *Red Rag*, 1978

Caplan, P. and Bujra, J.M. *Women United, Women Divided*, London; Tavistock, 1978

Clarke, T. and Clements, L. *Trade Unions Under Capitalism*, London; Fontana, 1977

Clegg, H.A. *The System of Industrial Relations in Great Britain*, Oxford; Blackwell 1972

Coote, A. 'Calling for positive action' in *New Statesman*, 16 March, 1979

Coote, A. 'Equality: a conflict of interest' in *New Statesman*, 31 August, 1979

Counter Information Services *Women Under Attack*, London; C.I.5 Anti-report, No. 15, 1976

Davies, R. *Women and Work*, London; Arrow, 1975

Donovan *Royal Commission on Trade Unions and Employers' Associations*, London; H.M.S.O., Cmnd. 3623, 1968

Drake, B. *Women in Trade Unions*, London; Labour Research Department, 1920

Dromey, J. and Taylor, G. *Grunwick: the workers' story*, London; Lawrence & Wishart, 1978

Edelstein, J.D. 'An Organizational Theory of Union Democracy' in *American Sociological Review*, No. 32 (i), February, 1967

Eisenstein, Z.R. (ed.) *Capitalist Patriarchy and the Case for Socialist Feminism*, New York; Monthly Review Press, 1979

Equal Opportunities Commission *Research Bulletin*, Vol. 1, No. 1, Manchester; E.O.C., Winter 1978-79

Equal Opportunities Commission *I want a baby . . . but what about my job?*, Manchester; E.O.C., March, 1979

Flanders, A. *Trade Unions*, London; Hutchinson, 1963

Fletcher, R. 'Trade Union Democracy: Structural Factors' in *Trade Union Register*, 1970 (ed.) Coates, K., Barratt Brown, M. and Topham, A., London; Merlin, 1970

Fryer, R.H., Fairclough, A.J. and Manson, T.B. 'Facilities for Female Shop Stewards: the British Protection Act and Collective Agreements' in *British Journal of Industrial Relations*, Vol. 16, 1978

Fryer, R.H., Fairclough, A.J. and Manson, T.B. *Organisation and Change in the National Union of Public Employees*, London; NUPE, 1974

Fryer, B., Fairclough, A. and Manson, T. 'Notes: Employment and Trade Unionism in the Public Services' in *Capital and Class*, Conference of Socialist Economists, No. 4, Spring, 1978

Gardiner, J. 'Women in the Labour Process and Class Structure' in *Class and Class Structure* (ed.) by Hunt, A., London; Lawrence and Wishart, 1977

Goldthorpe, J.H. *The Affluent Worker, Industrial Attitudes and Behaviour*, London; Cambridge University Press, 1968

General and Municipal Workers' Union *Equality at Work — The Way Forward*, Esher; G.M.W.U., 1976

Hakin, C. *Sexual divisions within the labour force: occupational segregation*, Department of Employment Gazette, November, 1978

Harrison, M. *Women in ASTMS*, Warwick University, 1980

Hartman, H.I. 'The Unhappy Marriage of Marxism and Feminism: towards a more progressive Union' in *Capital and Class*, Conference of Socialist Economists, No. 8, Summer, 1979

Hebden, J. 'Men and Women's Pay in Britain 1968-75' in *Industrial Relations Journal*, Vol. 9, No. 2, 1978

Beveridge, W. *Report on the Social Insurance and Allied Services*, London; H.M.S.O., Cmnd. 6404, 1942

Hughes, J. *Trade Union Structure and Government Research Papers 5 (ii)*, Royal Commission in Trade Unions and Employers' Associations, HMSO, 1968

Hunt, J. *Organising Women Workers*, London; Workers' Educational Association, 1976

Hurstfield, J. *The Part Time Trap*, London; Low Pay Unit, 1978

Hyman, R. *Strikes*, London; Fontana, 1972

Jackson, M.P. *Industrial Relations: a textbook*, London; Croom Helm, 1977

Joreen 'The Tyranny of Structurelessness' in *Radical Feminism,* (ed.) Koedt, A., Levine, E., Rapone, A., New York; Quadrangle, 1973

Kuhn, A. and Wolpe, A.M. *Feminism and Materialism: Women and Modes of Production*, London; Routledge and Kegan Paul, 1978

Labour Research *TUC Women's Conference*, London; Labour Research Department, May, 1977 and May, 1978

Labour Research *Women at Work*, London; Labour Research Department, December, 1978

Labour Research, *Women in Trade Unions*, London; Labour Research Department, March, 1979

Lawrence, E. *Women Workers and Trade Unions, Progress Report*, Newcastle-upon-Tyne Polytechnic, September, 1977

Lewenhak, S. *Women and Trade Unions*, London; Ernest Benn, 1977

Lewenhak, S. *Women and Work*, London; Macmillan, 1980

Lockwood, D. *The Blackcoated Worker*, London; Allen and Unwin, 1958

Lumley, R. *White Collar Unionism in Britain*, London; Methuen, 1973

McCarthy, W.E.J. (ed.) *Trade Unions*, Harmondsworth; Penguin, 1972

McCarthy, W.E.J. *Making Whitley Work*, London; DHSS, 1976

Mackie, L. and Pattullo, P. *Women at Work*, London; Tavistock, 1977

Mitchell, H. *The Hard Way Up*, London; Virago, 1977

Moser, C.A. and Kalton, G. *Survey Methods in Social Investigation*, London; Heinemann, 1971

National Association of Local Government Officers *Working Party Report on Communications Between Headquarters, Districts and Branches and Membership Participation*, London; NALGO, 1976

National Association of Local Government Officers *Equal Rights Working Party Report*, London; NALGO, 1975

Nichols, T. and Armstrong, P. *Workers Divided*, London; Fontana, 1976

Nickell, S.J. 'Trade Unions and the Position of Women in the Industrial Wage Structure' in *British Journal of Industrial Relations* Vol. 15, 1977

Novarra, V. *Women's Work, Men's Work*, London; Marion Boyars, 1980

Oakley, A. *Housewife*, Harmondsworth; Penguin, 1977

Oakley, A. *Sex, Gender and Society*, London; Temple Smith, 1971

Oppenheim, A.N. *Questionnaire Design and Attitude Measurement*, London: Heinemann, 1966

Pinchbeck, I. *Women Workers and the Industrial Revolution 1750-1850*, London; Cass., 1969

Roberts, B.C., *Trade Union Government and Administration in Great Britain*, London; London School of Economics, 1956

Robinson, O. and Wallace, J. *Pay and Employment in Retailing*, Farnborough; Saxon House, 1976

Rowbotham, S. *Women's Consciousness, Man's World*, Harmondsworth; Pelican, 1974

Rowbotham, S., Lynne, S. and Wainwright, H. *Beyond the Fragments: Feminism and the making of socialism*, London; Merlin, 1980

Schreiner, O. *Women and Labour*, London; Virago, 1978

Sedley, A. *Part-time Workers Need Full-time Rights*, London; NCCL, 1980

Sloane, P. (ed.) *Women and Low Pay*, London; Macmillan, 1980

Smart, C. *Women, Crime and Criminology*, London; Routledge and Kegan Paul, 1976

Snell, M. 'The Equal Pay and Sex Discrimination Acts: Their impact in the workplace', in *Feminist Review*, Vol. 1, London, 1979

Soldon, N.C. *Women in British Trade Unions 1874-1976*, Dublin; Gill & Macmillan, 1978

Spender, D. *Man Made Language*, London; Routledge & Kegan Paul, 1980

Spinrad, W. 'Correlates of Trade Union Participation: A summary of the literature' in *American Sociological Review*, No. 25, July, 1960

Stageman, J. *Women in Trade Unions*, Hull University, 1980

Trades Union Congress *Positive Action: a discussion document*, London; TUC, 1980

Trades Union Congress *Women in the Trade Union Movement*, London; TUC, 1950

Trades Union Congress *Women Workers' Conference Report*, Nos. 43-50, London; TUC, 1973-80

Trade Union Research Unit *Technical Note 40*, Oxford; Ruskin College, November, 1977

Transport and General Workers' Union *Women's Rights in Industry*, London; TGWU, 1972

Union of Shop, Distributive and Allied Workers *Rights for Working Women*, Manchester; USDAW

Wainwright, H. 'Women and the Division of Labour' in *Work, Urbanism and Inequality*, (ed.) Croom Helm, 1978

Wertheimer, B.M. and Nelson, A.H. *Trade Union Women: a study of their participation in New York City Locals*, New York; Praeger, 1975

Westergaard, J. and Hennetta, R. (ed.) 'Women in the labour market' in *Class in a Capitalist Society: a study of contemporary Britain*, London; Heinemann, 1975

Wigram, M. *Survey of female manual workers in Tower Hamlets*, Polytechnic of Central London, 1980

Wilson, A. *Finding a Voice: Asian Women in Britain*, London; Virago, 1978

Wilson, E. *Women and the Welfare State*, London; Tavistock, 1977

Women's Studies Group Centre for Contemporary Cultural Studies *Women Take Issue: aspects of women's subordination*, London; Hutchinson, 1978

**❝ You cannot achieve socialism without reference to women: the two are inextricably mixed. We cannot have socialism without a very wide extension of women's rights. ❞**

*Jo Richardson MP*
*Annual Conference 1980*

The Labour Party has always believed that women should play a leading role in the political process and that they are still a long way from achieving this. We welcome this opportunity to offer you the chance to take an active part in the Labour Party.

- - - - - - - - - - - - - - - - ✂

# Membership Form

I wish to become a member of the Labour Party and I am prepared to pay a minimum subscription of £3.00 per annum (£5.00 from 1 January 1981).

I hereby declare that I accept the policy and programme of the Labour Party, that I am prepared to accept the Rules and Constitution of the Labour Party, and that I am not a member of any organisation ineligible for affiliation to the Labour Party.

**NAME** _____

**ADDRESS** _____

_____

**TRADE UNION** _____

**TELEPHONE No.** _____

**ARE YOU UNDER 25?** _____ **DATE** _____

**SIGNATURE** _____

NB. Your membership must be formally accepted by the Labour Party.

I,........................, finding myself bored stiff with the usual, run-of-the-mill press, declare that I want to read a paper that doesn't let the fat-cats sit around unharassed. A paper that remains radical and independent, shining a light of publicity on the doings of government, the City, big business and entrenched interests everywhere. A paper that ventures where others fear to tread. In short, I'd like to subscribe to the **NEW STATESMAN**. I realise that my £23* will bring me my weekly dose of fresh air for a year without my having to queue at the newsagent.

Address:-............................................

.................................................................

Begin my subscription from ................ I enclose £ ....

*UK rate only, as at Dec. 1980. Ring 01-405 8471 for foreign rates and up-to-date quote.

Subscriptions, New Statesman, 10 Great Turnstile, London WC1V 7HJ